BLOOMSBURY

VANESSA BELL

DESIGN FOR OMEGA BEDHEAD: A VASE OF FLOWERS. c.1917

DUNCAN GRANT

FIRESCREEN DESIGN. late 1912

BLOOMSBURY

THE ARTISTS, AUTHORS AND DESIGNERS BY THEMSELVES

EDITED BY GILLIAN NAYLOR

MITCHELL BEAZLEY

PREFACE

Since so much has been written by and about the members of the Bloomsbury Group, and since the painters involved were so prolific in their output, my main problem in compiling this book has been one of selection. As far as the illustrations are concerned, this is the most comprehensive survey of the painting and designs associated with the Group published to date, but there are, inevitably, omissions. The texts were equally difficult to select: I wanted, as far as possible, to 'tell a story', so that there is a certain narrative element in the extracts selected. At the same time, however, I felt it essential to concentrate on the development of the Group's aesthetic and social theories, and since both Clive Bell and Roger Fry were published extensively, here again I have had to be rigorously selective. I have kept, as far as possible, to a chronological framework within each section, although, in some cases, the positioning of the illustrations relates to the themes within each section rather than a strict regard for chronology.

I would like to thank Professor Quentin Bell and Angelica Garnett for their kind permission to reproduce paintings and to quote from extensive texts and memoirs. Henrietta Garnett was also very helpful in the gathering of picture material. I would also like to thank the Charleston Trust and Geraldine Guest and Christopher Naylor at Charleston for their permission to photograph there, and for their patience.

The Publishers would also like to thank all the other owners of copyright in the letters and memoirs used who have graciously allowed their publication. Strenuous efforts have been made to contact all the owners of the original letters, but one or two have proved elusive and to these our apologies are offered.

First published in Great Britain in 1990 by
Pyramid, an imprint of Reed Consumer Books Limited
Michelin House, 81 Fulham Road, London SW3 6RB
and Auckland, Melbourne, Singapore and Toronto

Reprinted by Mitchell Beazley,
an imprint of Reed Consumer Books Limited, 1993

ISBN 1 85732 243 6

A CIP catalogue record for this book is available from the British Library

Printed in China

Editors: Lewis Esson/Sarah Chapman
Art Director: Linda Cole
Designer: Adrian Morris
Picture researchers: Jessica Walton, Carol Varley
Production by Landmark Production Consultants

Front cover: Vanessa Bell, Design for Screen (detail), 1913–14
(Courtauld Institute Galleries, London), see plate 203 for full reproduction

Back cover: Duncan Grant, Vanessa Bell, c.1918
© The Duncan Grant Estate, 1978
(National Portrait Gallery, London)

CONTENTS

VANESSA BELL
THREE PAINTED TILES IN A WOODEN FRAME, 1920s

DUNCAN GRANT

HEAD OF VANESSA BELL IN A RED SCARF. 1917

INTRODUCTION

In spite of the many attempts to define and evaluate it, the 'Bloomsbury' phenomenon remains elusive. This is partly due to the fact that its representatives included writers, historians, economists, critics and artists, who all, in their separate fields, challenged certain inherited assumptions and values, values which were founded on an ideal of service, morality and order. As well as questioning the conventions of political economy, or of the novel, or of art, or indeed of sexual and personal relations, 'Bloomsbury' also challenged the traditions of historical and political interpretation. All the bastions of an assumed culture, therefore, were attacked by the inheritors of that culture: the children of judges and generals, scholars and intellectuals used, or misused, their privileges of birth and circumstance in order to demonstrate that absolutes and certainties could be merely conventions.

There were many dangers in these attitudes, not least those of isolation and disestablishment. Having challenged social as well as intellectual moralities, those associated with 'Bloomsbury' might well have been ostracized and ignored, at least by the establishment whose values they despised. But although their achievements, especially in the early years, were met with incomprehension and in some cases with rejection and derision, the group was sufficiently cohesive and confident, and, perhaps more significantly, sufficiently intellectually and financially independent, to survive the criticisms of the traditionalists. (Virginia Woolf is the exception: she had courage, as well as genius, but she was defenceless when confronted with criticism, whether real or assumed.) But the very qualities which united them made them vulnerable to attacks from innovators of their own generation, and from subsequent avant-gardes, who saw them as a small but influential social group which had succeeded in exercising a disproportionate amount of power in their wide areas of interest. The Hogarth Press, for example, could publish those writers (including Virginia Woolf) it chose to promote; Maynard Keynes, with the acumen to make money, could provide his friends with financial advice; and Roger Fry, or so it was alleged, used his influence to advance not only his ideologies, but his friends.

In the early years, however, the group seemed intellectually and socially non-conformist rather than malevolent. Such attitudes are of course a characteristic of youth, and, as so many of these writers indicate in their memoirs, the generation which came of age at the turn of the century felt itself at the dawn of a new era. As Virginia Woolf wrote in *A Sketch of the Past*: 'Two different ages confronted each other in the drawing room at Hyde Park Gate: the Victorian age; and the Edwardian age ... We were living say in 1910; they were living in 1860.' The sense of liberation on escaping from the family home is evident in most of the reminiscences quoted here: for although the older generation was liberal in several senses, their liberalism rarely challenged the primacy of the family and the rituals of social convention, rituals in which wives and daughters were expected to play a vital, although conformist role. Virginia, for example, claimed that she and Vanessa 'learned the Victorian game of manners so thoroughly that we have never forgotten them'.

Cambridge

The men were naturally expected to go to university, and then to follow a career: idleness and dilettantism formed no part of their inheritance, and these families, although affluent, did not enjoy the wealth of the aristocracy or the industrial entrepreneur (with the exception of Clive Bell, whose family had made a fortune from Welsh coal, and, as Vanessa was to find to her dismay, had its own, equally alienating rituals). But as the extracts in this book indicate, it was, at least for these sons of the professional intelligentsia, the experience of Cambridge at the turn of the century that was the formative influence on the development of the Bloomsbury ethos. It was at Cambridge that their friendships and philosophies were forged, and where these young men first began to enjoy the stimulation of intellectual as well as personal freedom.

Cambridge was the obvious choice of university for these sons of lawyers and men of letters: its undergraduates were trained for professional and public life, and, especially in colleges like King's and Trinity, intellectual enquiry was considered vital to education. According to Maynard Keynes, the teaching there maintained 'in direct succession the English tradition of Locke and Berkeley and Hume, of Mill and Sidgwick, who in spite of their divergences of doctrine, are united in a preference for what is a matter of fact, and have conceived their subject as a branch of science rather than of the creative imagination . . .' (Preface to *A Treatise on Probability* 1921).

Cambridge, then, was a stronghold of Utilitarianism, the enlightenment philosophy associated with Jeremy Bentham and John Stuart Mill. This was a philosophy of moral and social commitment, founded in concepts of reason, progress and belief in the perfectibility of man. Utilitarianism posited the 'Greatest Happiness Principle' — or the conviction that, in the words of Mill in his book *Utilitarianism* (1861), 'actions are right in proportion as they tend to promote happiness, wrong as they tend to promote the reverse of happiness'. Such ideals, however, did not imply a hedonistic pursuit of pleasure: the aim was collective happiness, it being the duty both of the individual and the state to promote the welfare of the greatest number. Fundamental to these developing concepts of Utilitarianism was the conviction that the 'good' was quantifiable, and that the objective methods of science could be used both to define and to achieve it.

These ideas and ideals were adapted and challenged by subsequent Utilitarian thinkers (including Leslie Stephen and John Neville Keynes), but the belief in duty and the work ethic survived: work was seen as an end in itself rather than as a pursuit of personal wealth (contempt for luxury was an inherited characteristic of the Bloomsbury group). At the same time, such a philosophy could absorb a range of religious attitudes, from the Quaker beliefs of the Fry family to the rationalism and agnosticism of the Stephens; and the nature as well as the purpose of the 'good' was constantly questioned and redefined.

When Roger Fry won a scholarship to study natural sciences at King's College in 1885, Cambridge (although very different from 'Bloomsbury's' Cambridge at the turn of the century) was a revelation to him. Cambridge represented freedom, friendship, and above all talk; Fry found colleagues there who supported his growing lack of sympathy with his family's religious and political beliefs. He shared rooms with his school-friend John McTaggart, who was to become a lecturer in moral sciences at Trinity, and who had already, as a schoolboy, alarmed

INTRODUCTION

Fry's parents with his atheism. Fry's great friend was 'Goldie' — Goldsworthy Lowes Dickinson (soon to be appointed a Fellow of King's), and they celebrated their new-found and no doubt innocent hedonism by spending nights under the stars talking of nature and poetry and 'hearing all the birds wake up one after another'. 'I never was so happy in my life before', he wrote to his mother in 1887.

In the same letter he told his mother that he had been initiated as an Apostle, a member of that exclusive debating society which, it was claimed, did more to 'educate' its members than the University's academic curriculum. The society, according to a former member, was dedicated to 'the pursuit of truth with absolute devotion and unreserve ... The gravest subjects were continually debated, but the gravity of treatment ... was not imposed, though sincerity was'. The Apostles demanded of its 'brothers', therefore, intellect, intelligence and wit, and the society promoted long-lasting — and sometimes notorious — friendships and loyalties (Anthony Blunt and Guy Burgess were Apostles in the 1930s). When Roger Fry was elected to the society in the 1880s political convictions were important, but they were founded in Utopian rather than revolutionary socialist ideals. Fry may well have planned to entertain 'Socialists' in his room in the family home, in order to 'plot the destruction of society till any hour of the night', but this was the radicalism of a generation inspired by William Morris rather than by Karl Marx.

One of the many undergraduate converts to Morrisian ideals was C.R. Ashbee, a friend of Goldsworthy Lowes Dickinson also at King's. Ashbee, who was to found his Arts and Crafts inspired Guild of Handicraft in the East End of London in 1888, was in his final year when Fry arrived. With their common concern for art, philosophy and philanthropy they became friends, Fry initially sharing Ashbee's (and the Morris generation's) conviction that art had a social as well as moral purpose. Even while he was at Cambridge, however, he was questioning these convictions. ' ... I do not think art is as simple as I used to think it', he was writing to Ashbee in 1886, 'I do not think we have been wont enough to lay stress on the value ... of pure aesthetics as apart from the emotional end. I am also still very much mixed about its relation to morality.' Such concerns were vital to Fry, since by this time he was determined to become a painter. His experiences, as well as his friendships at Cambridge, had given him the confidence to defy his parents' expectations that he should follow a scientific career. Such a decision, which required courage as well as conviction (qualities which Fry rarely lacked), also meant a degree of financial insecurity. Although his father provided him with an allowance for several years, Fry was generally short of money, particularly after his marriage in 1896. His wife, Helen Coombe, was a painter and stained-glass designer associated with A.H. Mackmurdo's Century Guild, a group of artist-craftsmen also inspired by Morrisian ideals. Two years after they were married, she suffered from her first attack of mental illness, and, in spite of remissions in the early years when their two children were born, and persistent efforts to find a cure, Helen was sent to a home for the mentally disabled (run by Quakers) in 1910. (When she died it was found that her illness was physical rather than mental — she was suffering from ossification of the cartilage of the brain.)

Vanessa Stephen (as she then was) recalls seeing 'two tall figures walking together, the woman perhaps taller than the man' in the Fellows' Garden at King's College, Cambridge in 1902 or 1903. 'Those are the Roger Frys', she was told. By this time Fry was making a reputation as an art connoisseur and scholar (although not, to his regret, as a painter). Soon after leaving Cambridge, with a First Class Honours degree, he travelled in Italy (a revelation) and studied painting in Paris (a disappointment). He was to travel frequently to Italy in these early years, making meticulous studies of early Italian art. These preoccupations and his research there seemed to initiate a promising career. Fry had published his first book — on *Giovanni Bellini* — in 1899, and he had met Bernard Berenson, whose encouragement he acknowledges in the preface. He was also writing for the *Athenaeum*, and in 1903 was appointed to the consultative committee of the newly formed *Burlington Magazine*.

A year later Fry made his first visit to the United States in order to raise funds for the *Burlington*, a commission that was to lead to his encounters with the American millionaire J. Pierpont Morgan, and the offer of a prestigious appointment (seemingly from within Morgan's gift) at the Metropolitan Museum of Art in New York. Something of the complexities of these negotiations and Fry's association with the museum (and its wealthy patron) is indicated in the extracts that follow. Fry was first invited to become Assistant Director, but was turned down when he asked for more money (Helen felt unable to travel, and he needed to pay for her treatment, as well as for the household in England). In 1906 he accepted the post of Curator of the Department of Paintings, which seemed to ensure him adequate time in Europe. When he was en route to the States, however, he received the offer of the Directorship of the National Gallery in London. Believing himself committed to the Metropolitan, he felt that he had to turn this down, thus destroying the possibility of continuing his career in England. His association with the Metropolitan lasted until 1910, and it was never an easy one. Fry was embroiled in problems of acquisition and attribution; he needed to balance what he felt should be the ideals of the museum with the autocratic and unpredictable demands of its patron, and he was constantly worried about his wife's health. When his appointment was finally terminated in 1910, Fry returned to England with no permanent work, but with a reputation for scholarship, taste and connoisseurship. His real battles, however, had only just begun, for he was about to destroy what recognition he had gained with new, and seemingly uncharacteristic, enthusiasms.

Although he had met Vanessa previously, Roger first got to know the 'Bloomsbury' group in 1908 or 1910 (1910 according to Clive Bell, 1908 according to Vanessa). Whatever the date, the occasion was memorable both for Clive and Vanessa. They met him in a train from Cambridge to London, and 'talk began and continued unceasingly'. 'Roger told me', wrote Clive Bell, ' . . . that he proposed to show the British the work of the newest French painters.' He found himself in the company of enthusiasts. Clive was embarking on his Great Book, to be called *The New Renaissance*, parts of which were eventually published as *Art* (1914) and *Civilization* (1928); and Vanessa was a painter impatient with the *status quo*.

Clive Bell, Leonard Woolf, Lytton Strachey, Thoby Stephen and Saxon Sydney-Turner had all gone up to Trinity College, Cambridge in 1899 (Maynard Keynes and E.M. Forster, 'that elusive colt of a dark horse' as Keynes was to call him, were at King's). With the exception of Clive Bell and Thoby Stephen, all were Apostles. Since the time of Fry's membership, however, the intellectual preoccupations of the society had been transformed by the philosophy of a new Fellow of Trinity, G.E. Moore ('the only great man whom I have ever met or known', according to the sober-minded Leonard Woolf, who had the opportunity to meet many great men). Several members of 'Old Bloomsbury' have described the lasting and liberating impact of Moore's ideas. According to Clive Bell, he freed his disciples 'from the ugly spell of a doctrine in which we had been reared: he delivered us from Utilitarianism', and for Maynard Keynes the experience was 'exciting, exhilarating, the beginning of a new renaissance, the opening of a new heaven on a new earth'.

George Moore was trained as a classicist, and had changed his subject to philosophy in his third year at Cambridge. In 1903 he published *Principia Ethica*, and it was this book, and perhaps more significantly 'the talk which preceded and followed it' (Keynes) which had so profound an effect upon his contemporaries. Moore's philosophy is frequently summed up by a quotation from the book's final chapter, on *The Ideal*: 'By far the most valuable things, which we can know or can imagine, are certain states of consciousness, which can be roughly described as the pleasures of human intercourse and the enjoyment of beautiful objects.' The relevance of such concerns to the emerging 'Bloomsbury' ethos is obvious. At the same time, however, this celebration of 'certain states of consciousness' did not necessarily imply a facile hedonism: Moore's emphasis on 'knowing and imagining' involved a personal as well as philosophical reinterpretation of the accepted conventions of individual and social morality. It involved a re-examination of the nature and meaning of the 'good', as well as of the nature of truth and reality; and the investigation of these concepts was pursued through rigorous attempts to define 'meaning'. Clive Bell was to relate these ideals to aesthetics, and his conviction (in *Art*) that 'there is no greater means to good than art' was an extension of the Cambridge debates at the turn of the century.

To this Cambridge generation, therefore, Moore's appeal lay in his 'clarity, freshness and common-sense', and his philosophies confirmed their rejection of Victorian values and conventions. His stress on 'the pleasures of human intercourse' emphasized the value of friendship, and also contributed to the exclusivity of the group, who had no time for the boring and the banal, or for what Virginia described as 'all that tremendous encumbrance of appearance and behaviour' (*Moments of Being*). Once initiated, their loyalties, however strained, lasted for life. These loyalties, of course, did not follow any conventional form, since sexual and marital orthodoxies were unimportant. Homosexuality was celebrated by the Apostles, and continued to be celebrated, discussed (and practised) by the apostolic succession in and beyond Bloomsbury. References to sex were no longer taboo, even in mixed company. 'We listened with rapt interest to the love affairs of the buggers. We followed the ups and downs of their chequered histories', Virginia wrote of the evenings in Gordon Square (*Moments of Being*). 'All this had the result that the old sentimental views of marriage in which we were brought up were revolutionized. I should be sorry to tell you how old I was before I saw that there is nothing shocking in a man's having a mistress, or in a woman's being one.' Clive Bell's affairs, and his long association with Mary Hutchinson, were thus accepted, as was Vanessa's with Duncan. (This makes the silence, within and beyond the family circle, about Angelica's true parentage difficult to understand; Angelica was not 'officially' told that Duncan was her father until she was 17, although it was a fact, as she reports in her autobiography *Deceived with Kindness*, that she had 'obscurely known for a long time'. But such seemingly crude and cruel silences indicate the survival of all too human inhibitions, even among this close-knit group that claimed to have no time for socially acceptable half-truths).

Early Bloomsbury

If Cambridge represented freedom for the men of the group, it was the death of Leslie Stephen, and his children's decision to move from the 'rich red gloom' of Hyde Park Gate to the 'light and air' of Bloomsbury that signalled the independence of Vanessa and Virginia Stephen. Vanessa, significantly enough, would have nothing to do with William Morris wallpapers, and painted the walls of the house in Gordon Square 'with washes of plain distemper' (*Moments of Being*). She and Virginia had rooms of their own there, and they emphasized their rejection of social convention by entertaining young men in the evenings. The girls' revolt, which to the older generation (as well as to many of their friends) hinted at immorality, was more shocking than that of the young men, and their choice of aristocratic friends was also considered injudicious, for they were taken up by Lady Ottoline Morrell whose lavish and eccentric entertainments at Garsington Manor were neither in keeping with the sobriety traditionally associated with the Stephens, nor with the expectations of the more conventional members of upper middle-class society. But it was their association with artists that brought wider notoriety. It was, of course, in order that Vanessa should study painting — it was part of her inheritance (on her mother's side) and a respectable pastime for a middle-class lady, both before and after marriage. Painting as a serious career and an obsession, however, was certainly not acceptable for a woman.

According to their reminiscences, the fact that Vanessa was to be a painter and Virginia a writer was determined during their childhood. Leslie Stephen encouraged his elder daughter's talent: she had drawing lessons as a child, and had found liberation from the oppressive atmosphere at Hyde Park Gate when she was allowed to attend a private art school in South Kensington (she was then seventeen). She was talented enough to be awarded a place in the Royal Academy Schools in 1901, and was initially impressed by the teaching there, especially that of John Singer Sargent. But her father's illness and family responsibilities prevented her from total commitment in these early years. She had read about the French Impressionists and was sufficiently impressed to go to a lecture about them, but she had few opportunities to see their paintings, and even less to study them. Like most of her young (and some of her older) contemporaries, she thought that the Royal Academy was reactionary and retrograde, and she supported the campaigns of the New English Art Club, which had been established in 1886, to break the control of the Academy and provide a focus for experiment and an alternative approach. Once she was free to concentrate on her own interests and to travel abroad, Vanessa began to emerge from her chrysalis. She made memorable visits to Italy and Paris a few months after her father's death, renewing her acquaintance with her brother's friend Clive Bell, who was spending a year in Paris (Clive had originally gone there to research a thesis on the Congress of Verona, but was more stimulated by the British community of painters he met who introduced him to the work of Matisse, Bonnard and Van Gogh, as well as by the exhibitions in the *Salon d'Automne* and *Les Indépendants*).

The freedom of Bloomsbury allowed Vanessa to establish her own routine as a painter, which she struggled to maintain throughout her life (with intermissions for childbirth, illness and mourning), and although she, like Duncan Grant, was later to distance herself from 'art politics', she began to submit work for exhibition. One of her earliest surviving portraits — of Lady Robert Cecil — was exhibited at the New Gallery in 1905, and in that same year she launched the 'Friday Club'. Initially a discussion group, prompted, no doubt, by the Bloomsbury Thursday evening gatherings and by the clubs and societies the young men enjoyed at Cambridge, the members included several of her women colleagues from the Royal Academy Schools and 'lay' members like Virginia, Adrian and Saxon Sydney-Turner. The club flourished; the painters began to organize regular exhibitions of their work, and by 1910 they had a permanent venue in the Alpine Club Gallery.

Between 1905 and 1910 several events had intensified Vanessa's determination to establish herself as a painter. In 1907, shortly after the death from typhoid of her brother Thoby, she married Clive Bell, whose preoccupation with art and knowledge of modern painting obviously impressed her. Their first son, Julian, was born in 1908, and by that time any isolation she may have felt as the only painter in the Bloomsbury Group was broken by the introduction of Duncan Grant into the circle, and by her growing friendship (and brief love affair) with Roger Fry, who in 1910 organized the first Post-Impressionist exhibition.

Duncan Grant, a cousin of Lytton Strachey, had trained as a painter at the Westminster School of Art and briefly at the Slade. He also studied in Paris (where he met Matisse, visiting his studio at Issy-les-Moulineaux where he saw an early version of Matisse's *La Danse*). He spent some time in Italy, and like Roger Fry some years earlier was impressed by Piero della Francesca's frescoes in Arezzo. The French painter Simon Bussy (who married Lytton Strachey's sister Dorothy) also gave him practical advice, encouraging him to work consistently and to study technique by copying Florentine paintings.

When Duncan began to frequent Bloomsbury towards the end of 1910, he had already exhibited at the New English Art Club, and his *Lemon Gatherers* (p78), which Vanessa bought was exhibited at the Friday Club. He had also painted several portraits, interiors and still lifes, and had begun studies for a series of murals for Maynard Keynes' room at King's College, Cambridge. Like Vanessa, he was experimenting with various genres, and his eclecticism, like hers, was characteristic of painters associated with the NEAC. Whereas before 1910 Vanessa concentrated her developing skills on portraits, still lifes, and interiors (*Iceland Poppies* for example, and *46 Gordon Square* (p96), with its complex abstraction of space and perspective), Duncan was confronting his recent experiences in France and Italy and extending his range of subject matter and technique. His preoccupation with mural painting is evident in the implied monumentality of the *Lemon Gatherers* and *Solomon and the Queen of Sheba* (p86), and their classicizing harmonies of form and colour also reflect the influence of the work of Puvis de Chavannes and Maurice Denis on British painters at this time. But his more experimental work — some of his sketches for the Cambridge murals, for example, and his *Head of Eve* (p85) — indicate the impact of his encounters with the avant-garde in France.

It was, however, the energy and commitment of Roger Fry that forced these young painters to redefine their personal and professional expectations. Fry, recently returned from his disappointments with the museum world in the States, was still a respected member of the art establishment in England. He was European advisor to the Metropolitan Museum in New York, and had been appointed Editor of the *Burlington Magazine* in 1910; he was consolidating his growing reputation for scholarship and connoisseurship, and he was also respected by New English Art Club painters such as William Rothenstein and Walter Sickert.

The Post-Impressionist Exhibitions

Fry's decision to mount a polemic exhibition of the work of painters such as Van Gogh, Gauguin, Vlaminck, Derain, Rouault, Picasso and Cézanne, was a deliberate challenge to the more reactionary members of the art establishment, and the furore roused by the First Post-Impressionist Exhibition is described in recollections of the events. But it was not only the bourgeoisie who were incensed: this show, and the Second Post-Impressionist Exhibition of 1912 also shattered the various avant-gardes in England with personal as well as ideological vendettas.

Fry had never confined himself to the role of historian, nor would he lay claim to objectivity in his assessments. He believed in a 'Great Tradition' in art, a tradition that had been shattered in the nineteenth century. 'I believe', he wrote in *The Nation* in November 1910, 'that it is not difficult to show that the group of painters whose work is on view at the Grafton Gallery are in reality the most traditional of any recent group of artists . . . they are in revolt against the photographic vision of the nineteenth century . . .'

This 'photographic vision' — the recreation or representation of an ideal of reality — characterized the painstaking work of the Pre-Raphaelites as well as the medievalizing idylls of their successors; but, perhaps more significantly, what Fry described as 'the exact and literal imitation of nature' was also the basis of the art of the Impressionists, and memories of the battle for the recognition of their ideals and achievements were still very much alive in Britain in 1910. Impressionism was avant-garde in England when Fry decided to become a painter; as a scientist, he was interested in their 'scientific evaluation of colour', but, as he reported in *Retrospect*, he 'came to feel more and more the absence in their work of structural design'. For 'structural design' (or Clive Bell's 'significant form') was, Fry believed, the one universalizing element that united all great painting. 'One chief aspect of order in a work of art is unity', he had written in *An Essay in Aesthetics* (1909), '. . . unity of some kind is necessary for our restful contemplation of the work of art as a whole, since if it lacks unity we cannot contemplate it in its entirety . . .'

It is interesting that Fry also refers in this essay to the work of Dr Denman Ross, an American painter, patron, theorist and Harvard professor, who had published his *Theory of Pure Design* in 1907. Fry had met Ross in the States, and was evidently impressed by his ideas on form, colour and the nature of perception; for such seemingly 'science'-based investigations not only confirmed his own conception of connoisseurship as evaluation of the 'work of art as a whole', but they also confirmed his dissatisfaction with contemporary associations of art with morality, and with any ideal of 'truth to nature'. 'Art', wrote Roger Fry in his *Essay in Aesthetics*, 'appreciates emotion in and for itself', and by describing emotion as an 'end in itself' Fry was acknowledging the theories of G.E. Moore, of which he would have already been aware both through his continuing association with The Apostles and his more recent acquaintance with Clive and Vanessa Bell.

The recognition of the 'universal in the particular' was, according to Fry and Bell, one of the prerogatives of the Post-Impressionist painters and, by that recognition, the Post-Impressionists were recovering what Fry described as 'the language of design': 'I tried in vain to explain what appeared to me so clear, that the modern movement was essentially a return to the ideas of formal design which had been almost lost sight of in the fervid pursuit of naturalistic representation' (*Retrospect*). The formal values of a painting, therefore, were more important than its subject matter, and any 'message' a great painting might convey transcended narrative, resemblance, and any form of associationism, moral or sentimental, to evoke a unique 'state of mind': 'All art depends upon cutting off the practical responses to sensations of ordinary life, thereby setting free a pure and as it were disembodied functioning of the spirit'. This was a credo that Clive Bell reinforced in his book *Art*, in which he evokes G.E. Moore's *Principia Ethica* to support his argument that 'creating works of art is as direct a means to good as a human being can practise. Just in this fact lies the tremendous importance of art: there is no more direct means to good.'

For Vanessa the impact of the exhibition was personal and practical rather than philosophical; she had succeeded in freeing herself from social conventions when she moved the family to Bloomsbury, and now she realized that there was nothing to stop her painting as she wanted to, rather than as her mentors thought she ought to. For her, there was ' . . . a sudden pointing to a possible path, a sudden liberation and encouragement to feel for oneself . . . Freedom was given one to be oneself.' She expressed this freedom in paintings such as *Studland Beach* (p105), *Frederick and Jessie Etchells Painting* (p104) and *The Tub* (p111); here the shapes and figures are uncompromisingly two-dimensional, simplified and abstracted so that the emphasis is on form and colour rather than on any overt narrative or representational content. Duncan Grant was already working towards a simplication of form and content, especially in his experiments for murals. His *Queen of Sheba* (p86), intended for a decorative scheme at Newnham College, Cambridge, uses what Vanessa describes as his 'leopard manner', with separate brushstrokes of colour creating a stippled effect. And as if to confirm the liberation, Roger Fry, whose vision was rarely matched by his achievement in painting, produced a series of landscapes (*Chauvigny* (p80) and *White Road with Farm* (p81) for example) which reflect his debt to Cézanne as well as his admiration for the work of his young friends. 'You're doing splendid things, damn you', he wrote to Vanessa in 1914, 'and mine will always be makeshift.'

In his introduction to the Second Post-Impressionist Exhibition, Fry spelled out the implications of this emphasis on form. 'The logical extreme of such a method', he wrote, 'would undoubtedly be the attempt to give up all resemblance to natural form, and to create a purely abstract language of form — a visual magic.' Fry related this 'visual magic' to the work of Picasso, and in 1913, when he included paintings by Kandinsky in an Alpine Club exhibition, he described his abstractions as 'pure visual music'. In their personal explorations of form and content, neither Fry, nor Bell, nor Duncan Grant sustained this 'logical extreme', although they did experiment with abstraction in a series of paintings in 1914–15. One of the most remarkable of these is Duncan Grant's 5-m (15-ft) *Abstract Kinetic Collage Painting with Sound* (p248), which was intended to be viewed 'cinematically' through a box, to the accompaniment of music by Bach.

Omega

It was this brief preoccupation with abstraction in fine art, however, that enabled the painters to challenge conventions in applied art when Roger Fry launched the Omega Workshops in 1913. Omega was to be involved with contemporary decorative art, and follow what Fry described as the 'normal custom of employing contemporary artists to design furniture and hangings'. His aim was first and foremost practical — to provide work and an income for impoverished young painters — but at the same time he was convinced, as he explained in a letter to Bernard Shaw, that 'the Post-Impressionist Movement is quite as definitely decorative in its methods as was the Pre-Raphaelite, and its influence on decorative design is destined to be as marked'. He did not follow Arts and Crafts precedents in assuming a moral or social role for Omega; and, in spite of the 'Morrisian' overtones of his *Art and Socialism* essay, he did not believe in a medieval or guild ideal of craftsmanship. The workshops were to maintain the 'progressive' tradition Fry had identified in fine art, and its precedents were French rather than English.

Fry had already worked with painters (including Duncan Grant and several of the original Omega team such as Frederick Etchells and Bernard Adeney) on a commission for murals in the student refectory at London's Borough Polytechnic in 1911, and the success of this collaborative effort convinced him that artists could work together on the same projects. The Omega work, therefore, was to be anonymous; the pay was modest, and following the opening at the Fitzroy Square premises, commissions began to trickle in. One of the first of these — from the *Daily Mail*, to design a sitting room for the 1913 Ideal Home exhibition — prompted a controversy which split the Omega apart, shattering all illusions of artistic goodwill and mutual endeavour. The 'Ideal Home Rumpus', as it came to be called, was led by Wyndham Lewis, who accused Fry of appropriating a commission intended for him and Spencer Gore and of plots to exclude Frederick Etchells from being represented in an independently organized exhibition.

The accusations and ripostes are set out in this book, and the repercussions still reverberate. But whatever the rights and wrongs of the case, the furore does give some indication of the personal antagonism that Fry and his colleagues could provoke, and continue to provoke, among the avant-garde as well as the traditionalists. And although the quarrel was based on professional rather than ideological issues, its bitterness is indicative of the rifts in aesthetic theory and practice among English painters at that time. Wyndham Lewis, unlike Roger Fry and his colleagues, formed part of a radical and confrontational avant-garde, and his Vorticist movement, inspired by Italian Futurism, was anti-traditional both in form and content. It was politically subversive in intention, it celebrated the machine and urban life, and since its purpose was to convey 'information and ideas' rather than 'aesthetic emotion' it was dismissed, at least by Clive Bell, as illustration rather than art.

The quarrel with Spencer Gore, on the other hand, underlined Fry's problems with an alternative radical tradition in British art — the 'social realism' associated with the Camden Town Group of painters which had been launched in 1911, with Gore as president. Walter Sickert, the group's 'elder statesman', had described 'the plastic arts' as 'gross arts, dealing joyously with gross material facts', and these painters were preoccupied with the working-class environment, the racecourse, the music-hall and contemporary urban life.

Given such preoccupations, the choice of subject matter was more important to them than problems of form; and although 'radical' when judged within the context of the Pre-Raphaelite-inspired symbolist tradition, this concentration on themes from contemporary life was in no way concerned with the Vorticists' celebration of technology and the machine. Fry could appreciate the painterly and textural qualities of such work but, given his admiration for French achievements and his belief in a progressive classical tradition based on the transcendental qualities of form, he would ultimately judge such painting as narrative, anecdotal and populist, and therefore of minimal significance in what he conceived as the Great Tradition of European Art.

Views on Art and Life

For Fry, then, all great art had a spiritual role to play in society, and this transcended both commentary and conventional morality. Such convictions meant that he had no time for alternative radicalisms in twentieth-century European art; Surrealism and Expressionism, for example, were 'the revenge of Germany', and the psychological unease that they engendered had nothing to do with the traditional and spiritually redemptive role of art.

Ideas such as these made Fry's own development as a painter problematic to him, since his ideals constantly challenged his achievement. There are conceptual as well as aesthetic changes in his painting, and these are most obvious during the period when he was organizing the Post-Impressionist exhibitions and the Omega Workshops. It was then that he experimented with collage and abstraction and, like Vanessa Bell and Duncan Grant, discovered the liberating potential of colour. This liberalization is most evident in his landscapes, which are a complete negation not only of his academic training but also of both the English and the Impressionist tradition. He also experimented with the representation of form, as well as with the selection of subject matter, but could never entirely realize the force of his convictions in his own paintings. 'I am painting hard at landscapes', he wrote to his sister Margery in June 1918, ' . . . I think some good, but I can't take the next step which will be my inevitable synthesis, and not a willed and deliberate one.'

Although he worked at being a painter throughout his career, Fry was never entirely satisfied with his work, and towards the end of his life he felt totally alienated from contemporary developments in art. In September 1932 he wrote to Charles Mauron: 'I find myself more and more in the mood of . . . the Dutch landscapists of the seventeenth century . . . I have entirely ceased to belong to my age and I find myself more and more disappointed by the academic results of the Cubists and others — ultimately the avant-gardisme seems to me more and more nugatory.'

Fry's struggles to define and demonstrate an aesthetic in his own paintings also made for ambiguities in his attitudes to the work of his friends. Whereas Clive Bell had no inhibitions in his published assessments of Duncan Grant ('the best English painter alive', he wrote in his review of Duncan's first one-man exhibition in 1920), Roger Fry was more circumspect. In the *Living Painters* series (1923), Fry considered Grant more successful as a decorator than as a painter: 'The effort to create complete and solidly realized constructions in a logically

DUNCAN GRANT
LITTLE URN, c.1933

coherent space, which has succeeded of late to the more decorative conception that derived from Gauguin, has, I think, hampered rather than helped his expression', he wrote.

The problem here lay in the criteria on which Fry based his assessment. He could only judge his own and his contemporaries' work in the light of the revelations he had received from French art in the years leading up to the First World War, and for Fry the messages were first and foremost theoretical. But neither Duncan Grant nor Vanessa Bell were preoccupied with theory; they equated the French achievement with a liberation from academic conventions, a liberation that sanctioned new explorations of colour, form, tone and line, and which gave Vanessa the freedom to be herself, so that in the years leading up to and during the First World War their work was both radical and innovative.

Their retreat to Charleston, however, and their personal association marked their retirement from 'art politics'. This was to a certain extent a retreat into a private world, although their life was enviably cosmopolitan — they spent a great deal of time in London and in 'the Second Charleston in France', the Bells' house in Cassis — and they could afford to travel and keep up with contemporary developments. They exhibited, and maintained their friendships with painters, but neither was prepared, or needed, to fight for fame or ideologies. They both painted obsessively, but they painted for themselves rather than for an audience — Duncan Grant, according to Roger Fry, never did 'a single stroke of work with a view to ingratiate himself'. They painted their immediate world — home, family, friends, garden and landscape — a personal iconography which was extended to the decoration of the house itself.

Neither Duncan Grant nor Vanessa Bell would have claimed that this work was challenging in any ideological sense; the goals they set themselves were self-imposed, involving a personal vision of colour, light and space, and a very personal sense of place. Their painting is lyrical rather than confrontational, and its concern for private rather than public issues isolates it from mainstream developments. And their designs, too, were far from mainstream: their work for Omega was inventive and innovatory, and although they did continue with 'decorative design' in later years (textiles for Allan Walton, for example, and ceramics), they rarely engaged in the current debates on art and industry. They painted and decorated a local church (pp300—303), produced sets for ballets (pp304—305), and continued to decorate friends' houses, but their schemes for *The Queen Mary*, the most prestigious of their public commissions, were rejected.

It is therefore ironic that these two artists are perhaps more widely known today for their talents as decorators than for their achievements as painters. This latter-day celebration coincided with the rehabilitation of Charleston, that very private refuge. Charleston, once an isolated and eccentric retreat, is now open to the public, and if any of it's visitors ask 'What was Bloomsbury?' they might be provided with a few tentative clues. Charleston is a place where people lived, talked, worked, read and painted. But the paintings do not keep their conventional place . . . they are of course, on the walls throughout the house, but they are also on the doors, on beds, tables, boxes and screens, on lampshades, trays and pottery; they cover the sides of the baths, and frame the fireplaces. Charleston, therefore, celebrates individuality and the degentrification of the bourgeois ideal of the country house. William Morris had created his own 'Palace of Art' half a century earlier, but the role of art had now changed: these artists did not set out to change the world, but to create their own. Their friends and associates may have made more impact as thinkers, writers and iconoclastic biographers, and they certainly made more enemies, but the painters were involved with private rather than public concerns.

In their retreat from confrontation and from convention, Vanessa Bell and Duncan Grant demonstrated the ambiguities of that 'sense of values' which is central to Clive Bell's concept of civilization. Clive Bell's *Civilization* is a plea for an intellectual meritocracy, with the freedom to enjoy 'pleasures and desires, standards and values . . . different from those of the busy multitude'. It is based on a naïve belief in progress, the triumph of reason, and the good life of the mind sustained by decent wine and well-cooked food. ('. . . in the end', observed Virginia Woolf, 'it turns out that Civilization is a lunch party at 50 Gordon Square'.) First published in 1928, it ignored social, political and economic realities, and the next Bloomsbury generation was among the first to condemn it: '. . . we had no hesitation', wrote Quentin Bell, '. . . in telling Old Bloomsbury that it had taken the wrong turning . . . that it acquiesced in a social system which it knew to be wrong and allowed itself to become part of the Establishment.' Julian Bell's premature death in the cause of political commitment shattered this world, and the values they were left with were the familiar ones of work, love and friendship, values that need no rhetoric to sustain them. But let us leave the last word to Virginia Woolf:

Where they seem to me to triumph is in having worked out a view of life which was not by any means corrupt or sinister or merely intellectual; rather ascetic and austere indeed; which still holds, and keeps them dining together, and staying together, after twenty years; and no amount of quarrelling, or success, or failure, has altered this. Now I do think that this is rather creditable. But tell me who *is* Bloomsbury in your mind?

VANESSA BELL
TILE DESIGN, AUTUMN c. 1950

WHAT IS BLOOMSBURY?

AS THESE EXTRACTS INDICATE, 'BLOOMSBURY' DEFIES DEFINITION. THERE IS NO DOUBT THAT THERE WAS SUCH A 'THING', AS CLIVE BELL WAS DRIVEN TO CALL IT; THERE IS ALSO NO DOUBT THAT THOSE INTIMATELY INVOLVED WITH IT FELT THEMSELVES TRAVESTIED AND MISINTERPRETED, BOTH BY THE 'OUTSIDE WORLD' (A CONSISTENT OFFENDER) AND FROM WITHIN.

The original 'Bloomsberries' could only think of themselves as friends with certain common interests, and with the tensions and rivalries common to all long-standing friendships. How could such a group of friends, therefore, with concerns as varied as politics and economics, art and literature, constitute a 'group', represent a doctrine, or put forward any consistent challenge? They could not, after all, agree among themselves — a characteristic, as Clive Bell points out, of most friendships — so it is perhaps inevitable that most of these extracts concentrate on what Bloomsbury was not: 'we were not proselytizers, missionaries, crusaders, or even propagandists', wrote Leonard Woolf.

At the same time, however, it is obvious that the 'Bloomsberries' were attacked, or admired, for what they represented: they were, or seemed to be, an intellectual élite, with inherited privileges that enabled them to ignore social and moral conventions and challenge traditional assumptions about scholarship, art and literature. They were so endowed with gifts that it was all too easy for them to parade their sense of values — values that were considered dubious by the reactionary as well as by the avant-garde. It is no wonder, therefore, that these are for the most part defensive statements. By 1956 when Clive Bell wrote his polemic, his 'civilization' was a lost cause: the 'brisk young fellows' of the next generation paraded their 'distressing accents', and young artists were finding totally unexpected significance in American consumer culture. 'Bloomsbury', whatever it was, was bewildered; but its causes survive.

VANESSA BELL

TEA THINGS, 1913

22

WHAT IS BLOOMSBURY?

Quentin Bell, Bloomsbury, *1968*

    . . . Bloomsbury was always under fire. This is the common fate of all groups, coteries and cliques, particularly if they have sufficient liveliness to make a new contribution to the thought of their time. If that contribution has been connected with the arts, then contemporary reactions are likely to be very hostile and the aftermath of success is likely to be depreciation. Art lives by destroying itself and, as fashions change, artists and their works grow, fade, and sometimes grow again in public estimation. Bloomsbury certainly has not been exempt from these variations of aesthetic feeling and today its situation is not unlike that of the Pre-Raphaelites forty years ago. Bloomsbury however was unlike the Pre-Raphaelities in that it has been criticized from a bewilderingly large number of points of view . . .

Leonard Woolf, Beginning Again, An Autobiography of the Years 1911 to 1918, *1964*

    . . . What came to be called 'Bloomsbury' by the outside world never existed in the form given to it by the outside world. For 'Bloomsbury' was and is currently used as a term — usually of abuse — applied to a largely imaginary group of persons with largely imaginary objects and characteristics . . .

. . . There have often been groups of people, writers and artists, who were not only friends, but were consciously united by a common doctrine and object, or purpose artistic or social. The utilitarians, the Lake poets, the French impressionists, the English Pre-Raphaelites were groups of this kind. Our group was quite different. Its basis was friendship, which in some cases developed into love and marriage. The colour of our minds and thought has been given to us by the climate of Cambridge and Moore's philosophy, much as the climate of England gives one colour to the face of an Englishman while the climate of India gives a quite different colour to the face of a Tamil. But we have no common theory, system, or principles which we wanted to convert the world to: we were not proselytizers, missionaries, crusaders, or even propagandists . . .

Clive Bell, 'Bloomsbury', *from* Old Friends, *1956*

    There is mystery in the word, and money too perhaps. Or is it merely for fun that grave historians and pompous leader-writers no less than the riff-raff of Fleet

Street and Portland Place chatter about the thing? 'The thing', I say, because that is the least committal substantive I can think of, and it is not always clear whether what the chatterers are chattering about is a point of view, a period, a gang of conspirators or an infectious disease. Beyond meaning something nasty, what do they mean by 'Bloomsbury'? . . .

. . . The name was first applied to a set of friends by Lady MacCarthy — Mrs Desmond MacCarthy as she then was — in a letter: she calls them 'the Bloomsberries'. The term, as she used it, had a purely topographical import; and the letter . . . must have been written in 1910 or 1911. But the story begins earlier. It begins . . . in October 1899 when five freshmen went up to Trinity — Cambridge, of course — and suddenly becoming intimate, as freshmen will, founded a society as freshmen almost invariably do. It was a 'reading society' which met in my rooms in the New Court on Saturdays at midnight, and here are the names of the five original members: Lytton Strachey, Sydney-Turner, Leonard Woolf, Thoby Stephen, Clive Bell. After he had gone down, and after the death of his father, Thoby Stephen lived at 46 Gordon Square, Bloomsbury, with his brother Adrian and his two sisters Vanessa (later Vanessa Bell) and Virginia (later Virginia Woolf). These two beautiful, gifted and completely independent young women, with a house of their own, became the centre of a circle of which Thoby's Cambridge friends were what perhaps I may call the spokes. And when, in 1907, the elder married, the circle was not broken but enlarged; for Virginia, with her surviving brother Adrian, took a house in nearby Fitzroy Square: thus, instead of one *salon* — if that be the word — there were two *salons*. If ever such an entity as 'Bloomsbury' existed, these sisters, with their houses in Gordon and Fitzroy Squares, were at the heart of it. But did such an entity exist?

All one can say truthfully is this. A dozen friends . . . between 1904 and 1914 saw a great deal of each other. They differed widely . . . in opinions, tastes and preoccupations. But they liked, though they sharply criticized, each other, and they liked being together. I suppose one might say they were 'in sympathy' . . . Anyhow the first World War disintegrated this group, if group it were, and when the friends came together again inevitably things had changed . . .

. . . Thoby Stephen had died in the late autumn of 1906. Leonard Woolf was in Ceylon between 1904 and 1911: remained in Bloomsbury Lytton Strachey (who, in fact, lived in Hampstead), Saxon Sydney-Turner, Clive Bell. There were the two ladies. Add to these Duncan Grant, Roger Fry, Maynard Keynes, H. T. J. Norton and perhaps Gerald Shove, and I believe you will have completed the list of those of the elder generation who have been called 'Bloomsbury'. Certainly Desmond and Molly MacCarthy and Morgan Forster were close and affectionate friends, but I doubt whether any one of them has yet been branded with the fatal name. So much for the old gang.

As I have said, after the war a few men of a younger generation became intimate with most of us . . . First and foremost come David Garnett and Francis Birrell, both of whom we — by 'we' I mean the old Bloomsberries — had known and liked before 1914. Immediately after the war, by a stroke of good luck, I made the acquaintance of Raymond Mortimer; and about the same time Lytton Strachey, lecturing at Oxford, met Ralph Partridge. I think it may have been through Francis Birrell that we came to know a brilliant girl from Newnham, Frances Marshall (later Mrs Ralph Partridge) . . .

WHAT IS BLOOMSBURY?

... Naturally, with time and space at their familiar task, the bonds of sympathy loosened — though I think they seldom snapped — and so the friends of 'the twenties' were even less like a group than the friends of the pre-war period ... For beyond mutual liking they had precious little in common, and in mutual liking there is nothing peculiar. Yes, they did like each other; also they shared a taste for discussion in pursuit of truth and a contempt for conventional ways of thinking and feeling — contempt for conventional morals if you will. Does it not strike you that as much could be said of many collections of young or youngish people in many ages and many lands? ...

... I have done my best to name those people who certainly were friends and of whom some at any rate have often been called 'Bloomsbury'. I have suggested that the people in my list held few, if any, opinions and preferences in common which were not held by hundreds of their intelligent contemporaries: I emphasize the words 'in common'. Wherefore, if my list be correct, it would seem to follow that there can be no such thing as 'the Bloomsbury doctrine' or 'the Bloomsbury point of view' ...

... There are other critics, of whom I know as little as they appear to know of the reputed pillars of Bloomsbury, who hold a clean contrary opinion. I write from hearsay; but I am told there are brisk young fellows, authorities on the 'twenties', whose distressing accents are sometimes heard on the wireless by those who can stand that sort of thing, who explain that in 'the twenties' there still existed in England a gang or group which for years had devoted itself to stifling, or trying to stifle, at birth every vital movement that came to life. Oddly enough this gang, too, goes by the name of Bloomsbury. Now who can these baby-killers have been? Obviously not Roger Fry who introduced the modern movement in French painting to the British public, nor Maynard Keynes, who, I understand, revolutionized economics. Nor does it seem likely that the critics are thinking of Lytton Strachey who, far from being reactionary, went out of his way to help the cause of Women's Suffrage when that cause was reckoned a dangerous fad, or of Leonard Woolf who was a Fabian long before British socialism had become what the Americans call a racket. Whom can these castigators of 'Bloomsbury' have in mind? Clearly not Virginia Woolf who invented what amounts almost to a new prose form; nor, I hope, certain critics who, long before 1920, had appreciated and defended the then disconcerting works of Picasso and T. S. Eliot.

Once more I cry aloud: Who were the members of Bloomsbury? For what did they stand? In the interests of history, if common decency means nothing to them, I beseech the Bloomsbury-baiters to answer my questions; for unless they speak out and speak quickly social historians will have to make what they can of wildly conflicting fancies and statements which contradict known facts. Thus, disheartened by the impossibility of discovering opinions and tastes common and peculiar to those people who by one authority or another have been described as 'Bloomsbury', the more acute may well be led to surmise that Bloomsbury was neither a chapel nor a clique but merely a collection of individuals each with his or her own views and likings. When to this perplexity is added the discovery that no two witnesses agree on a definition of the 'Bloomsbury doctrine', historians are bound to wonder whether there ever was such a thing. At last they may come to doubt whether 'Bloomsbury' ever existed. And did it?

FOUNDATIONS

'WHO WAS I THEN? ADELINE VIRGINIA STEPHEN ... DESCENDED FROM A GREAT MANY PEOPLE, SOME FAMOUS, OTHERS OBSCURE; BORN INTO A LARGE CONNECTION, BORN NOT OF RICH PARENTS, BUT OF WELL-TO-DO PARENTS, BORN INTO A VERY COMMUNICATIVE, LITERATE, LETTER-WRITING, VISITING, ARTICULATE LATE NINETEENTH-CENTURY WORLD ...'

DUNCAN GRANT

VANESSA BELL IN A RED DRESS, 1915

So wrote Virginia Woolf in *Moments of Being*. With one exception, this was the inheritance of the group of friends who began to 'drift in' to the house in Gordon Square, Bloomsbury, in the summer of 1905. (The exception was Clive Bell, whose family, according to his son Quentin, 'drew its wealth from Welsh mines, and expended it upon the destruction of wild animals'.) The inheritance, therefore, was intellectual rather than aristocratic: this was a dynasty of writers, scholars, scientists, judges, administrators, and in the case of Lytton Strachey and Duncan Grant, who were cousins, the army. As well as being 'communicative' and 'literate', they were energetic and hard-working, their dedication to the Victorian work ethic being based on an ideal of personal responsibility rather than private ambition. And although inevitably and essentially patriarchal, these dynasties drew much of their strength and individuality from the women, the Fry and several of the Strachey sisters achieving their own claim to eminence. In fact, as one perceptive historian of Bloomsbury has pointed out, 'there may be, person for person, more distinguished women in the families of Bloomsbury than there were distinguished men'. (S.B. Rosenbaum, *Victorian Bloomsbury*).

The brief descriptions of childhood given here, therefore, reveal both the freedoms and conventions of this late Victorian liberal tradition: Roger Fry, for example, was encouraged by his Quaker family to find both entertainment and instruction in the 'useful arts', Leonard Woolf's mother encouraged her children to read 'good' books; while Virginia and Vanessa Stephen were taught at home, Virginia teaching herself Greek and reading most of the Victorian novelists aloud while Vanessa painted. The members of the Bloomsbury Group were prone to autobiography, and for the most part their accounts recall a happy childhood. At Hyde Park Gate, however, where the Stephen family lived, 'darkness and silence' prevailed after the death of Julia Stephen in 1895. Vanessa was sixteen, and Virginia, then thirteen, had her first breakdown. Their half-sister Stella took on the role of mother, but she died shortly after her marriage in 1897. Their brothers could of course escape the darkness and their father's despair at school and at university, but since Vanessa and Virginia were girls, and the daughters of Leslie Stephen, any hope of such freedom was denied them.

The liberation of Cambridge life, even to so confident and intellectually secure a generation, is obvious in the following extracts (its implications are more fully discussed in the Introduction). 'Bloomsbury' ideals were forged at Cambridge at the turn of the century, and consolidated in the Thursday evening talks (and silences) at Gordon Square. Gordon Square was the antithesis of Hyde Park Gate: there the walls were painted white, everyone had a room of their own, and 'everything was on trial'.

But the shock of bereavement again destroyed this new-found equilibrium: in 1906, following a family visit to Greece, Thoby Stephen died from typhoid fever. Two days later, Vanessa, who had earlier refused to marry Clive Bell, announced her engagement to him; they were married in February 1907, and a year later their first child Julian was born.

The power of the past

VANESSA STEPHEN, 1905

Virginia Woolf, Roger Fry, A Biography, *1940*

When Roger was a child, the old hair-dresser who had cut Coleridge's hair was still cutting hair and recalling the poet's loquacity — 'He *did* talk!' he would say . . . A reading society met once in three weeks to read aloud selections from standard works' . . . Sometimes the society met at the Frys', and the leading spirit — Charles Tomlinson, F.R.S. — an indefatigable and erudite gentleman whose published works range from *The Study of Common Salt* to translations from Dante and Goethe . . . would drop in of a Sunday evening and listen to Sir Edward [Fry, Roger's father] reading aloud *Paradise Lost* or George Fox's *Journals* or one of Dean Stanley's books to the children. The reading over, Mr Tomlinson would talk delightfully, if incomprehensibly, to the children. And then he would invite them to tea with him. He would show them all the marvels of his 'den'. The small room, as befitted the multiplicity of its owner's interests, was crowded with fascinating objects. There was an electrical machine; musical glasses; and Chladni's clamp — an invention by which sand, when a violin was played, formed itself into beautiful patterns. Roger's life-long delight in scientific experiments must have been stimulated. But science was part of the home atmosphere; art was 'kept in its place', that is the Academy would be dutifully visited; and a landscape, if it faithfully recorded the scene of a summer holiday, would be dutifully bought. Thus it was

through Charles Tomlinson perhaps that he first became aware of those aesthetic problems that were later to become so familiar. As the author of a *Cyclopaedia of Useful Arts* Mr Tomlinson had access to certain factories, and he would take the little Frys with him on visits to Price's Candle Factory, Powell's Glass-making Works, and a diamond-cutting factory in Clerkenwell. 'And these factory visits', wrote Roger's sister Agnes, 'raised questions of a fresh sort; what made good art and bad art, what ornament was justified, and whether diamonds were not better used for machinery than for necklaces. He was very strongly of opinion that they were — a brooch, he told us, might be useful, but lockets were an abomination to him.' Roger's opinion, as to what made good and bad art, was unfortunately not recorded . . .

Leonard Woolf, Sowing, An Autobiography of the Years 1880 to 1904, *1960*

. . . I was eleven when my father died. I admired him greatly and certainly thought that I was fond of him, and I think that he was both fond and proud of me, because as a small boy I was intelligent, reserved, and had a violent temper, and so in fact resembled him. He was certainly intelligent, reserved, and quick-tempered, but also very nervous and highly strung, and, though normally very kind, more intolerant of fools and their folly than almost any other man whom I have known . . .

. . . My mother was a good-looking young woman and we all liked to see her let down her hair, for it reached well below her knees and was extraordinarily thick. She must have been a perfect wife for she adored my father and yet was sufficiently different from him to make life interesting always for both of them . . . The best hours of the day were between tea-time and my father's return from the Temple, for we spent them with her in the library playing, when we were quite small, and being read to later on when we were seven or eight or more . . .

. . . At home, my mother encouraged us from an early age to read 'good' books, Scott, Dickens, Thackeray, but it is a remarkable fact that until the age of sixteen, when at St Paul's I got into A. M. Cook's form, none of my teachers . . . ever suggested to me that it was possible to read a work of literature or other serious book for pleasure . . .

Vanessa Bell, Notes on Virginia's Childhood, a memoir, *1974*

. . . I cannot remember a time when Virginia did not mean to be a writer and I a painter. It was a lucky arrangement, for it meant that we went our own ways and one source of jealousy at any rate was absent.

Our happiest afternoons were spent in a small room handed over to us, opening from the large double drawing room. It was a cheerful little room, almost entirely made of glass, with a skylight, windows all along one side looking on to the back garden, a window cut in the wall between it and the drawing room, and a door (also half window) opening into the drawing room. Also another door by which one could retreat to the rest of the house. In this room we used to sit, I painting and she reading aloud. We read most of the Victorian novelists in this way, and I can still hear much of George Eliot and Thackeray in her voice . . .

PART I

The day mother died in 1895 — that $\frac{37}{\underline{5}}$ 42 years ago: & I
remember it — at the moment, watching Dr Seton walk away up Hyde Park Gate in the early
morning with his head bowed, his hands behind his back. Also the doves swooping. We had
been sent up to the day nursery after she died; & were crying. And I went to the open window
& looked out. It must have been very soon after she died, as Seton was then leaving the
house. How that early morning picture has stayed with me! What happened immediately
afterwards I can't remember . . .

Virginia Woolf, Reminiscences *from* Moments of Being, *1976*

. . . Another influence was even then astir in her [Vanessa], the
influence of an affection only to be gratified by people. No hole dug in the gardens however
deep, so that it was possible to extract clay of a malleable quality from it, gave her all that she
needed. Dolls did not satisfy her. At present, until she was fifteen indeed, she was outwardly
sober and austere, the most trustworthy, and always the eldest; sometimes she would lament
her 'responsibilities'. Other children had their stages, and sudden gifts and failings; she

VIRGINIA STEPHEN AND JULIAN BELL

seemed to draw on steadily, as though with her eye on some far object, which attained, she might reveal herself. She was very silent . . . But beneath the serious surface . . . there burnt also the other passion, the passion for art. She drew indeed under the care of a Mr Cook, but talk of art, talk of her own gifts and loves, was unknown to her. What did she think then? For with her long fingers grouping, and her eye considering, she surely painted many pictures without a canvas. Once I saw her scrawl on a black door a great maze of lines, with white chalk. 'When I am a famous painter —' she began, and then turned shy and rubbed it out in her capable way. And when she won the prize at her drawing school, she hardly knew, so shy was she, at the recognition of a secret, how to tell me, in order that I might repeat the news at home. 'They've given me the thing — I don't know why.' 'What thing?' 'O they say I've won it — the book — the prize you know.' She was awkward as a long-legged colt . . .

. . . So your mother [Virginia is writing the memoir for Julian Bell], whose sight seemed in some ways so clear, took it upon her to be what people call 'practical' though a generous talent for losing umbrellas and forgetting messages showed that nature sometimes delighted to laugh at the pretence. But the power which was not feigned and was probably recognized by those who trusted her, was what I call variously sagacity, and common sense, and more rightly perhaps, honesty of mind. She might not see all, but she would not see what was not there . . .

. . . She looked so self-contained, and so mature that clearly she would never act foolishly; but also there was so much promise of thought and development in eye and brow, and passionate mouth, that it was certain she would not long stay quiescent. The calm of the moment was as an instinctive shield to cover her wounded senses; but soon they would collect themselves and fall to work upon all these difficult matters so lavishly heaped upon them — and with what result?

She was beautiful, but she had not lived for eighteen years without revealing that she was also strong of brain, agile and determined; she had revealed so much in the nursery, where she would meet Thoby in argument, and press on to the very centre of the matter, whether it were question of art or morality. She was also, on her secret side, sensitive to all beauty of colour and form; but she hid this, because her views did not agree with those current around her, and she feared to give pain. Again, she was as quick to detect insincerity of nature as fallacy of argument, and the one fared as ill with her as the other; for her standard was rigid. But then she was bound to certain people by a kind of instinctive fidelity, which admitted of no question; it was, if anything, too instinctive . . . If her mother had lived it is easy to imagine how Vanessa, questing about her, like some active dog, would have tried one experiment after another, arguing, painting, making friends, disproving fallacies, much to her mother's amusement; she would have delighted in her daughter's spirit and adventures, mourned her lack of practical wisdom, and laughed at her failures, and rejoiced in her sense. But that is one of the things, which though they must have happened, yet, incredible though it seems, never did happen, death making an end of all these exquisite preparations. Instead Vanessa was first baffled by her mother's death, and the unnatural life which for a time was entailed upon us, and now again, Stella's [Vanessa and Virginia's half-sister's] death set her among entirely new surroundings . . .

PART I

Vanessa Bell, Hyde Park Gate, (a memoir), n.d.

        . . . Darkness and silence seemed to me to have been the chief characteristic of the house in Hyde Park Gate. If we did not read at meals like the Stracheys, we hardly talked. My father could only be spoken to through a tube and if it was shy work doing this in front of the family it was worse with strangers there. Then his sighs and groans needed accounting for, or so one felt, to almost any visitor and even when accounted for did not lead to cheerfulness. At dinner in the evening faces loomed out of the darkness like Rembrandt portraits and when 3 or 4 years later, I came to know Charles Furse and stayed with them in the country, one of the chief excitements of doing so was the bare plaster walls and faces seen against them . . .

Virginia Woolf, Reminiscences from Moments of Being, 1976

        . . . It thus came about that Nessa and I formed together a very close conspiracy. In that world of many men, coming and going, we formed our private nucleus. There we were, alone, with father all day. In the evening Adrian would come back from Westminster; then Jack [Hills] from Lincoln's Inn; then Gerald [Duckworth] from Dent's or Henrietta Street; then George [Duckworth] from the Post Office or the Treasury; and Thoby would be at Clifton or at Cambridge. The staple day would be a day spent together. And therefore we made together a small world inside the big world. We had an alliance that was so knit together that everything (with the exception of Jack perhaps) was seen from the same angle; and took its shape from our own vantage point. Very soon after Stella's death [1897] we saw life as a struggle to get some kind of standing place for ourselves in this [illegible]. We were always battling for that which was always being interfered with, muffled up, snatched away. The most imminent obstacle and burden was of course father . . .

Over the whole week . . . brooded the horror of Wednesday. On that day the weekly books were shown him. If they were over eleven pounds, that lunch was a torture. The books were presented. Silence. He was putting on his glasses. He had read the figures. Down came his fist on the account book. There was a roar. His vein filled. His face flushed. Then he shouted 'I am ruined.' Then he beat his breast. He went though an extraordinary dramatization of self-pity, anger and despair. He was ruined — dying . . . tortured by the wanton extravagance of Vanessa and Sophie [the cook]. 'And you stand there like a block of stone. Don't you pity me? Haven't you a word to say to me?' and so on. Vanessa stood by his side absolutely dumb. He flung at her all the phrases — about shooting Niagara and so on — that came handy. She remained static. Another attitude was adopted. With a deep groan he picked up his pen and with ostentatiously trembling fingers wrote out the cheque. This was wearily tossed to Vanessa. Slowly and with many groans the pen, the account book were put away. Then he sank into his chair and sat with his head on his breast. And then at last, after glancing at a book, he would look up and say half plaintively, 'And what are you doing this afternoon, Ginny?'

Never have I felt such rage and such frustration. For not a word of my feeling could be expressed . . . If Thoby had presented those books or George, the explosion would have been suppressed. Why had he no shame in front of women? . . .

Vanessa Bell, Hyde Park Gate, (a memoir), n.d.

         . . . What an aggravating young woman I must have been! For my only way of dealing with the situation was silence. I simply waited until the cheque was signed, unable to think of anything to say, acutely unhappy and rather terrified and knowing one couldn't pretend there was any special reason which wouldn't occur again for extra expenses that week *. . .*

Virginia Woolf, A Sketch of the Past from Moments of Being, 1976

         . . . Here of course, from my distance of time, I perceive what one could not then see — the difference of age. Two different ages confronted each other in the drawing room at Hyde Park Gate: the Victorian Age; and the Edwardian Age. We were not his children, but his grandchildren *. . .* The cruel thing was that while we could see the future, we were completely in the power of the past. That bred a violent struggle. By nature, both Vanessa and I were explorers, revolutionists, reformers. But our surroundings were at least fifty years behind the times *. . .*

Vanessa Bell, Hyde Park Gate (a memoir), n.d.

         . . . Our manner of spending our time when we started life again that autumn [following the deaths of her mother and half-sister] was not very different from what it had been before the catastrophe. Virginia went off to her room to read — and I went as I had already been doing for some time to Mr Cope's School of Art in South Kensington. I bicycled off in a large floppy hat which came off at draughty cross-roads, and a long skirt, the only danger coming from quick little butchers' or bakers' carts trotting sharply round corners *. . .*

   When I got into the grubby, shabby, dirty world of art-students at S. Kensington I wanted nothing else in the way of society. They were separate in every way from my home life and so a great relief. They knew no more about my private life than I knew about theirs and in their company one could forget oneself and think of nothing but shapes and colours and the absorbing difficulties of oil paint *. . .*

Virginia Woolf, A Sketch of the Past from Moments of Being, 1976

         Vanessa, I suppose, under the eye of Val Prinsep [a painter, and a relative of the Stephens] or [Walter William] Ouless or occasionally [John Singer] Sargent, painted from the life — she would bring home now and then very careful pencil drawings of Hermes perhaps, and spray them with fixative; or an oil head of a very histrionic looking male nude. And for the same three hours I would be reading perhaps Plato's *Republic*, or spelling out a Greek chorus. Our minds would escape to the world which on this November morning of 1940 she inhabits at Charleston and I in my garden room at Monks House. Our clothes would not be much different. She wore a blue painting smock; I perhaps a blouse and skirt. If our skirts were longer, that would be the only difference. Forty years ago she was rather tidier, rather better dressed than I. The change would come in the afternoon. About 4.30 Victorian society exerted its pressure. Then we must be 'in'. For at 5 father must be given his tea. And we must be better dressed and tidier, for Mrs Green was coming; Mrs H. Ward was coming; or Florence Bishop; or C. B. Clarke; or . . . We would have to sit at that table, either she or I, decently dressed, having nothing better to do, ready to talk . . .

  We both learned the rules of the Victorian game of manners so thoroughly that we have never forgotten them . . .

Cambridge: a new heaven on a new earth

Virginia Woolf, Roger Fry, A Biography, *1940*

  . . . He [Roger Fry] was working hard; he was showing brilliant promise as a scientist. But it was not the work in lecture-rooms or in laboratories that was most important to him. It was his talk with his friends. Lowes Dickinson, the young Fellow of King's, had quickly become the most important of those friends. All one hot moonlight night they sat and talked 'while a great dome of pale light travelled round from West to East and the cuckoo and the nightingale sang', and for a few hours 'we cared only for the now which is the same thing as being eternal'. His new friends were forcing him to take stock of the vague religious and political beliefs which he had brought with him from home and from Clifton . . .

Roger Fry To C. R. Ashbee   *Failand House, 18 October 1886*

  . . . There is a standard of beauty somewhere, and if there is not, the sooner we chuck the whole business the better. Just as to a morally-minded person it is inconceivable that there is not a right and a wrong absolutely, to which we constantly approximate, so to the artistically-minded man it is inconceivable that we have not got something at which we constantly aim. This is the result of some discussions with a certain poet Robert Bridges who has been staying here, a most delightful man. It was great fun hearing him uphold the standard of Beauty against my sceptical parents, and it has cleared my views much. He (R. B.) is very great on the severity of art and the necessity of enormous study on the technical parts without the least subordinating the higher aims to the technique . . .

Roger Fry To Lady Fry   *Cambridge, 26 May 1887*

  Since I last wrote I have been partially initiated into the society [The Apostles] I mentioned before, i.e. I have seen the records, which are very interesting, containing as they do the names of all the members which includes nearly everyone of distinction who was at Cambridge during the last fifty years. Tennyson, I think I told you, is still a member and there are references to the society in *In Memoriam* which none but the duly initiated can fully understand. Thompson, the late Master of Trinity, Baron Pollock, Lord

Derby, Sir James Stephen, Clerk-Maxwell, Henry and Arthur Sidgwick and Hort are all (or have been) members, so that I feel much awed by thus becoming a member of so distinguished and secret a society . . .

Roger Fry To C. R. Asbbee   *Cambridge, 21 November 1887*

. . . The phenomenal manifestations and emanations of the Devil or arch-genius of ugliness are many; but few for completeness and harmoniousness of general effect beat a certain house in Bayswater which I am now privileged to call my home.

It is huge and palatial, the outside being covered with blackish yellow-grey stucco which is moulded into the form of gigantic worm casts which are divided up in the shape and semblance of stones. But of the inside I will not speak: suffice it to say that it is a consummate conception carried out at enormous cost in sham marble stucco ormolu and gilt. In fact it is an Elysium which I fancy must be haunted by the spirits of all dead builders who are their own architects. Well, I went home for the Sunday to this place and was very wretched all day thinking of what might be going on further east. . . .

Roger Fry To Sir Edward Fry   *Cambridge, 21 February 1888*

Middleton has been very kindly advising me about my prospects in life, and I will try and give you as clear an account as I can of what he thinks. I explained to him (thinking it an extremely important factor) how unpleasing an idea it was to you that I should take up art. He says he quite understands the feeling that to fail in art is much more complete a failure and leaves one a more useless encumbrance on the world than to fail in almost anything else . . . so that he thinks, as you do, that unless I have a strong feeling I ought not to attempt it . . . He advised me if I thought I felt strongly enough to ask you to let me try for about two years and by the end of that time he says that he thinks I shall be able to tell what my own capacities are and whether it will be worth my while going on. No one can at all tell before that. If by that time of probation I find I can do nothing worthy and do not progress, I ought to give it up . . . he says the best course would be for me to do at least the first year's drudgery at the cast and to do that up here at the Museum of Casts; spending some time on dissecting in the laboratory . . .

He says that the idea of the possibility of landscape-painting without figures is quite untenable — you must correct your drawing and colour on the figure as you see there more immediately when you go wrong. I then told him the objection you had to the nude — which he said was very natural tho' so far as his experience went it did not lead to bad results and was not so harmful as an ordinary theatre . . .

Virginia Woolf, Roger Fry, A Biography, 1940

. . . The immediate question was a practical one. A friend's letter summed it up. 'What', he asked, 'are you going to be?' The 'awful Tripos' provided what, to his parents at least, seemed a decisive answer. Almost casually in the postcript to a letter he told his mother that the 'examiners have honoured me by giving me a first; this is the more kind on their part as I neither expected nor deserved one. It was telegraphed to me at Norwich this morning by Dickinson.' . . .

Roger Fry To G. L. Dickinson   *Palace Houses, 24 January 1889*

    . . . I've just finished my first day's work with [Francis] Bate — it was quite as dull as I expected but not more so, and I think he teaches well — he has ideas — he teaches you more how to analyse your impressions than how to move your pencil and this seeems to me the right end to begin. But all this is technical rot to you. I'm going to have a room with a fire in it where I shall work my own wicked will and have Socialists all unbeknown to the rest of the family, and we can plot the destruction of society till any hour of the night . . .

Clive Bell, Old Friends, *1956*

    'Anyone can see you're a freshman, sir,' said the head porter at the Great Gate of Trinity. He was telling me, as tactfully as he deemed necessary, that to carry an umbrella when wearing a gown was contrary to custom. To soften the snub he made a little conversation designed to show that no one need feel the worse for a bit of advice from so knowing a man, and, indicating another gowned freshman who happened to be crossing the court, observed — 'You'd never think he was a general's son.' The general's son was Lytton Strachey. Though unbearded, already he had encouraged a weak brown moustache, which, with his lank dark hair, pincer eye-glasses, and long chin, added somehow to that air of flexible endlessness which was his prevailing physical characteristic. No: Lytton Strachey, at the age of twenty, did not look a head-porter's notion of a general's son . . .

    . . . He and I were, I believe, singular in our set, if not in the University, in that we took some interest in the visual arts. I am still surprised, and disconcerted maybe, on going into a modern don's rooms to find there a nice collection of contemporary paintings. It is so unlike the dear old days when an Arundel print or two represented the *ne plus ultra* of academic æstheticism. But Lytton and I, while still in *statu pupillari* if you please, once met by chance in the National Gallery and more than once in the Fitzwilliam . . . Philosophically we were dominated by [George] Moore, and politics we despised. Let politicians disport themselves at the Union, where such small fry looked big; we liked some of them well enough in a patronizing way . . .

Desmond MacCarthy, Memories, *1953*

    . . . My undergraduate days were over, and I was going down to Cambridge one November afternoon in 1901 to visit George Moore, the philosopher, who still had rooms in Neville's Court. It must have been that train which gets us up to Cambridge in time for dinner . . . There was on this occasion one other occupant of the carriage that I entered that afternoon. He [Clive Bell] was a youth with a noticeable head of wavy auburn hair, and that milk-white skin which often goes with it. I cannot visualize him completely, but

CLIVE BELL, 1910

I think I am safe in saying that he was dressed with careless opulence, and that he wore, flung open, a dark fur coat with a deep astrakhan collar . . .

He appeared to have a foot in two communities which, in the University, and indeed in the world itself, are separated from each other by as deep a trench as divides, say, Roman Catholics from the rest of mankind. He seemed to live, half with the rich sporting-set, and half with the intellectuals; and sure enough next day I found my host in a white hunting-stock and a dressing gown. His aspect was reminiscent of a sporting young man in a Leech picture at that delicious moment when he has pulled off his top-boots and is about to take his hot shower-bath. That it was a Sunday and he could not have thrown a leg over a horse that morning, added to his character a touch of fantasy, which was in harmony with my first impression of him.

J. M. Keynes, My Early Beliefs, 1949   9 September 1938

. . . I went up to Cambridge at Michaelmas 1902, and [George] Moore's *Principia Ethica* came out at the end of my first year. I have never heard of the present generation having read it. But, of course, its effect on *us*, and the talk which preceded and followed it, dominated, and perhaps still dominate, everything else . . . Moore himself was a puritan and precisian, Strachey (for that was his name at that time) a Voltairean, Woolf a rabbi, myself a nonconformist, [J.T.] Sheppard a conformist and (as it now turns out) an ecclesiastic, Clive a gay and amiable dog, Sydney-Turner a quietist, [R.G.] Hawtrey a dogmatist and so on . . . We did not see much of [E.M.] Forster at that time; who was already the elusive colt of a dark horse. It was only for us, those who were active in 1903, that Moore completely ousted McTaggart, Dickinson, Russell. The influence was not only overwhelming; but it was the extreme opposite of what Strachey used to call *funeste*; it was exciting, exhilarating, the beginning of a renaissance, the opening of a new heaven on a new earth, we were the forerunners of a new dispensation, we were not afraid of anything . . . Nothing mattered except states of mind, our own and others people's of course, but chiefly our own. These states of mind were not associated with action or achievement or with consequences. They consisted in timeless, passionate states of contemplation and communion, largely unattached to 'before' and 'after' . . .

. . . We were among the last of the Utopians, or meliorists as they are sometimes called, who believe in a continuing moral progress by virtue of which the human race already consists of reliable, rational, decent people, influenced by truth and objective standards, who can be safely released from the outward restraints of convention and traditional standards and inflexible rules of conduct, and left, from now onwards, to their own sensible devices, pure motives and reliable intuitions of the good . . .

In short, we repudiated all versions of the doctrine of original sin, of there being insane and irrational springs of wickedness in most men. We were not aware that civilization was a thin and precarious crust erected by the personality and the will of a very few, and only maintained by rules and conventions skilfully put across and guilefully preserved. We had no respect for traditional wisdom or the restraints of custom . . .

. . . If, therefore, I altogether ignore our merits — our charm, our intelligence, our unworldliness, our affection — I can see us as water-spiders, gracefully skimming, as light and reasonable as air, the surface of the stream without any contact at all with the eddies and currents underneath . . .

Leonard Woolf, Sowing, An Autobiography of the Years 1880 to 1904, *1960*

. . . The intellectual, when young, has always been in all ages enthusiastic and passionate and therefore he has tended to be intellectually arrogant and ruthless. Our youth, the years of my generation at Cambridge, coincided with the end and the beginning of a century which was also the end of one era and the beginning of another. When in the grim, grey, rainy January days of 1901 Queen Victoria lay dying, we already felt that we were living in an era of incipient revolt and that we ourselves were mortally involved in this revolt against a social system and code of conduct and morality which, for convenience sake, may be referred to as bourgeois Victorianism . . .

. . . I also met Thoby's two sisters, Vanessa and Virginia Stephen, when they came up to see him. The young ladies — Vanessa was twenty-one or twenty-two, Virginia eighteen or nineteen — were just as formidable and alarming as their father, perhaps even more so. I first saw them

one summer afternoon in Thoby's rooms; in white dresses and large hats, with parasols in their hands, their beauty literally took one's breath away, for suddenly seeing them one stopped astonished and everything including one's breathing for one second also stopped as it does when in a picture gallery you suddenly come face to face with a great Rembrandt or Velasquez or in Sicily rounding a bend in the road you see across the fields the lovely temple of Segesta. They were at that time, at least upon the surface, the most Victorian of Victorian young ladies ... Vanessa and Virginia were also very silent and to any superficial observer they might have seemed demure. Anyone who has ridden many different kinds of horses knows the horse who, when you go up to him for the first time, has superficially the most quiet and demure appearance, but, if after bitter experience you are accustomed to take something more than a superficial glance at a strange mount, you observe at the back of the eye of this quiet beast a look which warns you be very, very careful. So too the observant observer would have noticed at the back of the two Miss Stephens' eyes a look which would have warned him to be cautious, a look which belied the demureness, a look of great intelligence, hypercritical, sarcastic, satirical ...

Virginia Woolf, A Room of One's Own, *1929*

... I found myself walking with extreme rapidity across a grass plot. Instantly a man's figure rose to intercept me. Nor did I at first understand that the gesticulations of a curious-looking object, in a cut-away coat and evening shirt, were aimed at me. His face expressed horror and indignation. Instinct rather than reason came to my help; he was a Beadle; I was a woman. This was the turf; there was the path. Only the Fellows and Scholars are allowed here; the gravel is the place for me. Such thoughts were the work of a moment. As I regained the path the arms of the Beadle sank, his face assumed its usual repose, and though turf is better walking than gravel, no very great harm was done ...

What idea it had been that had sent me so audaciously trespassing I could not now remember. The spirit of peace descended like a cloud from heaven, for if the spirit of peace dwells anywhere, it is in the courts and quadrangles of Oxbridge on a fine October morning ... As chance would have it, some stray memory of some old essay about revisiting Oxbridge in the long vacation brought Charles Lamb to mind ... Lamb then came to Oxbridge perhaps a hundred years ago. Certainly he wrote an essay — the name escapes me — about the manuscript of one of Milton's poems which he saw here. It was *Lycidas* perhaps, and Lamb wrote how it shocked him to think it possible that any word in *Lycidas* could have been different from what it is. To think of Milton changing the words in that poem seemed to him a sort of sacrilege ... It then occurred to me that the very manuscript itself which Lamb had looked at was only a few hundred yards away, so that one could follow Lamb's footsteps across the quadrangle to that famous library where the treasure is kept ... but here I was actually at the door which leads into the library itself. I must have opened it, for instantly there issued, like a guardian angel barring the way with a flutter of black gown instead of white wings, a deprecating, silvery, kindly gentleman, who regretted in a low voice as he waved me back that ladies are only admitted to the library if accompanied by a Fellow of the College or furnished with a letter of introduction.

That a famous library has been cursed by a woman is a matter of complete indifference to a famous library. Venerable and calm, with all its treasures safely locked within its breast, it sleeps complacently and will, so far as I am concerned, so sleep for ever. Never will I wake those echoes, never will I ask for that hospitality again, I vowed as I descended the steps in anger . . .

Old Bloomsbury: everything on trial

Virginia Woolf, Old Bloomsbury *from* Moments of Being, *1976*

. . . Vanessa had wound up Hyde Park Gate once and for all. She had sold; she had burnt; she had sorted; she had torn up. Sometimes I believe she had actually to get men with hammers to batter down — so wedged into each other had the walls and the cabinets become. But now all the rooms stood empty. Furniture vans had carted off all the different belongings . . . And Vanessa — looking at a map of London and seeing how far apart they were — had decided that we should leave Kensington and start life afresh in Bloomsbury.

It was thus that 46 Gordon Square came into existence. When one sees it today, Gordon Square is not one of the most romantic of the Bloomsbury squares. It has neither the distinction of Fitzroy Square nor the majesty of Mecklenburgh Square. It is prosperous middle class and thoroughly mid-Victorian. But I can assure you that in October 1904 it was the most beautiful, the most exciting, the most romantic place in the world . . . The light and the air after the rich red gloom of Hyde Park Gate were a revelation. Things one had never seen in the darkness there — Watts pictures, Dutch cabinets, blue china — shone out for the first time in the drawing room at Gordon Square. After the muffled silence of Hyde Park Gate the roar of traffic was positively alarming . . . But what was even more exhilarating was the extraordinary increase of space. At Hyde Park Gate one had only a bedroom in which to read or see one's friends. Here Vanessa and I each had a sitting room; there was the large double drawing room; and a study on the ground floor. To make it all newer and fresher, the house had been completely done up. Needless to say the Watts-Venetian tradition of red plush and black paint had been reversed; we had entered the Sargent-Furse era; white and green chintzes were everywhere; and instead of Morris wall-papers with their intricate patterns we decorated our walls with washes of plain distemper. We were full of experiments and reforms. We were going to do without table napkins . . . we were going to paint; to write; to have coffee after dinner instead of tea at nine o'clock. Everything was going to be new; everything was going to be different. Everything was on trial . . .

Vanessa Bell, Notes on Bloomsbury (Memoir Club), *1951)*

. . . We knew no one living in Bloomsbury then and that I think was one of its attractions . . . Then there was the Slade in Gower Street to which I went as an art student for a short time; but to me Professor Tonks, then in control, was a most depressing master. I made no friends there and soon left. It seemed as if in every way we were making a new beginning in the tall clean rather frigid rooms, heated only by coal fires in the old

fashioned open fireplaces. It *was* a bit cold perhaps, but it was exhilarating to have left the house in which had been so much gloom and depression, to have come to these white walls, large windows opening on to trees and lawns, to have one's own rooms, be master of one's own time, have all the things in fact which come as a matter of course to many of the young today but so seldom then to young women at least . . .

. . . Soon after this beginning in Gordon Square, I think in the summer of 1905, Thoby, not long down from Cambridge and now reading for the Bar, began to gather round him such of his Cambridge friends as were also starting life in London. It seemed to him a good plan to be at home one evening a week and though I do not think it had at first occurred to him to include his sisters in the arrangement, still there they were. So it happened that one or two of his Cambridge friends began to drift in on Thursday evenings after dinner. The entertainment was frugal. I believe there was generally some whisky to be had but most of us were content with cocoa and biscuits . . . It seemed as if, as soon as our very innocent society got under way and began to have some life in it, hostility was aroused. Perhaps this always happens. Any kind of clique is sneered at by those outside it as a matter of course and no doubt our ways of behaviour in our own surroundings were sufficiently odd, according to the customs of the day, to stir criticism. Certainly I remember being questioned curiously by a group of young and older people at an ordinary conventional party as to whether we really sat up talking to young men till all hours of the night? What did we talk about? – Who were these young men? etc. They laughed, even then there was a tone of disapproval.

What *did* we talk about? The only true answer can be anything that came into our heads. Of course the young men from Cambridge were full of the 'meaning of good'. I had never read their prophet G. E. Moore, nor I think had Virginia, but that didn't prevent one from trying to find out what one thought about good or anything else. The young men were perhaps not clear enough in their own heads to mind trying to get clearer discussions with young women who might possibly see things from a different angle. At any rate talk we all did, it's true, till all hours of the night. Not always, of course about the meaning of good – sometimes about books or paintings or anything that occurred to one . . .

Vanessa Stephen to Clive Bell   *[8 November 1906]*

. . . I wish that if you decide to go away, you would work at something. I don't mean that I in the least want you to go in for any particular profession, in fact I can't imagine you being a successful barrister or man of business! – but I do think you would be happier and would most likely think less of the Stephen family if you were producing some kind of work and not only adding to your knowledge. Besides I think brains are so badly wanted that people who possess them haven't the right to let them be of no use. I haven't the courage to go on being impertinent . . .

Virginia Woolf, Old Bloomsbury *from* Moments of Being, 1976

. . . It never struck me that the abstractness, the simplicity which had been so great a relief after Hyde Park Gate were largely due to the fact that the majority of the young men who came there were not attracted by young women. I did not realize that love, far from being a thing they never mentioned, was in fact a thing which they seldom ceased to discuss. Now I had begun to be puzzled. Those long sittings, those long silences, those long arguments ... They still excited me much more than any men I met with in the outer world of dinners and dances — and yet I was, dared I say it or think it even? intolerably bored. Why, I asked, had we nothing to say to each other? Why were the most gifted of people also the most barren? Why were the most stimulating of friendships also the most deadening? Why was it all so negative? Why did these young men make one feel that one could not honestly be anything? The answer to all my questions was, obviously — as you will have guessed — that there was no physical attraction between us ...

Vanessa Bell, Notes on Bloomsbury, *1951*

... Holidays in the country interrupted Thursday evenings and made a change from Bloomsbury. Its earliest chapter was very short — from the summer of 1905 to the autumn of 1906. Then after a holiday in Greece social evenings and our small circle generally seemed crushed by the tragedy of Thoby's death of typhoid fever at the age of twenty-six. He had seemed essential to the life and structure of our circle, but in youth, I suppose, no one is essential. The young mercifully recover from any blow and though it was true that life was changed for us yet something began to revive.

Then Clive Bell and I were married in the spring of 1907; that and the fact that in those terrible weeks such friends as Lytton and Saxon had become closer and more intimate helped a new life to begin. So when Virginia and Adrian moved from Gordon Square to Fitzroy Square in the spring of 1907 leaving us, a newly married couple, in Gordon Square they began fairly soon to have Thursday evenings again ...

Leonard Woolf, Beginning Again, An Autobiography of the Years 1911 to 1918, *1964*

... There had certainly been a profound revolution in Gordon Square. I had dined in 46 Gordon Square with Thoby and his two sisters, the Misses Stephens, in 1904 only a few days before I left England for Ceylon. Now seven years later in the same rooms meeting again for the first time Vanessa, Virginia, Clive, Duncan, and Walter Lamb I found that almost the only things which had not changed were the furniture and the extraordinary beauty of the two Miss Stephens. Vanessa was, I think, usually more beautiful than Virginia. The form of her features was more perfect, her eyes bigger and better, her complexion more glowing. If Rupert [Brooke] was a goddess's Adonis, Vanessa in her thirties had something of the physical splendour which Adonis must have seen when the goddess suddenly stood before him. To many people she appeared frightening and formidable, for she was blended of three goddesses with slightly more of Athene and Artemis in her and her face than of Aphrodite. I myself never found her formidable, partly because she had the most beautiful speaking voice that I have ever heard, and partly because of her tranquillity and quietude. (The tranquillity was to some extent superficial; it did not extend deep down in her mind, for there in the depths there was also an extreme sensitivity, a nervous tension which had some resemblance to the mental instability of Virginia) ...

FOUNDATIONS

Duncan Grant, 'Virginia Woolf', Horizon III, June 1941

I first knew Virginia Stephen when she and her brother Adrian took No. 29 Fitzroy Square, soon after her sister Vanessa married Clive Bell . . .

I had taken for a studio two rooms on the second floor of a house on the same side of the square. There was certainly not much gentility left in the district; the only relic of grandeur was a beadle to march round the square and keep order among the children, in a top-hat and a tail-coat piped with red and brass buttons. The Stephens were the only people I remember who had a complete house there; complete with their cook Sophie Farrell, their maid Maud, a front-door bell and a dog, Hans. A close friendship sprang up between Adrian Stephen and myself, and I had only to tap at the window of the ground-floor room to be let in. 'That Mr Grant gets in everywhere,' Maud once remarked to Virginia. But irregular as my visits were, in a sense they soon became frequent enough to escape notice . . .

Virginia Woolf, Moments of Being, 1976

. . . Here I come to a question which I must leave to some other memoir writer to discuss — that is to say, if we take it for granted that Bloomsbury exists, what are the qualities that admit one to it, what are the qualities that expel one from it? Now at any rate between 1910 and 1914 many new members were admitted. It must have been in 1910 I suppose that Clive one evening rushed upstairs in a state of the highest excitement. He had just had one of the most interesting conversations of his life. It was with Roger Fry. They had been discussing the theory of art for hours. He thought Roger Fry the most interesting person he had met since Cambridge days. So Roger appeared. He appeared, I seem to think, in a large ulster coat, every pocket of which was stuffed with a book, a paint box or something intriguing; special tips which he had bought from a little man in a back street; he had canvases under his arms; his hair flew; his eyes glowed. He had more knowledge and experience than the rest of us put together . . . The old skeleton arguments of primitive Bloomsbury about art and beauty put on flesh and blood. There was always some new idea afoot; always some new picture standing on a chair to be looked at, some new poet fished out from obscurity and stood in the light of day. Odd people wandered through 46 [Fitzroy Square]; Rothenstein, Sickert, Yeats, Tonks — Tonks who could, I suppose, make Vanessa miserable no more. And sometimes one began to meet a queer faun-like figure, hitching his clothes up, blinking his eyes, stumbling oddly over the long words in his sentences. A year or two before, Adrian and I had been standing in front of a certain gold and black picture in the Louvre when a voice said: 'Are you Adrian Stephen? I'm Duncan Grant.' Duncan now began to haunt the purlieus of Bloomsbury. How he lived I do not know. He was penniless. Uncle Trevor [Grant; uncle of Duncan and Lytton Strachey] indeed said he was mad. He lived in a studio in Fitzroy Square with an old drunken charwoman called Filmer and a clergyman who frightened girls in the street by making faces at them. Duncan was on the best of terms with both. He was rigged out by his friends in clothes which seemed always to be falling to the floor. He borrowed old china from us to paint; and my father's old trousers to go to parties in. He broke the china and he ruined the trousers by jumping into the Cam to rescue a child . . . Our cook Sophie called him 'that Mr Grant' and complained that he had been taking things again as if he were a rat in her larder. But she succumbed to his charm. He seemed to be vaguely tossing about in the breeze; but he always alighted exactly where he meant to . . .

Vanessa Bell, Notes on Bloomsbury, *1951*

... He [Duncan Grant] was penniless but seemed unaware of the fact. If he wanted to go from one place to another he would borrow the exact sum of 2½d perhaps, which any of us could afford. If he wanted a meal he appeared, and contributions from each plate were willingly made. So he solved the problem of living on air with satisfaction to everyone, and soon of course selling his pictures solved it even further. As he had a studio of kinds in Fitzroy Square it was easy for him to see a lot of Adrian and Virginia ... It was natural too that Maynard Keynes should become one of the circle and I think he very quickly felt at home in it.

Yet one more was to come, perhaps the most important of all — Roger Fry. Older than any of us, though that never seemed of the least importance, he had the advantage of greater experience of life and of art. But how one laughed at him and how ready he was to see the joke, how ready to discuss anything with the most ignorant of us ... Even now seventeen years after his death one is constantly surprised by the way in which those who knew him speak of him. English and French, both writers and painters, even those who were hardly grown up when he died, all seem to have been stirred by a deep affection and admiration and tell one how they still miss him. 'How honest he was. — He never minded admitting that he had been quite wrong and changing his mind if only he could come a little nearer the truth.' So someone who knew him well but who had never been a member of Bloomsbury said to me the other day. Not only did he bring himself to our circle, he knew many people both French

DUNCAN GRANT

and English who were strangers to us and he seemed to draw them to Bloomsbury, not as members necessarily but as delightful and sympathetic visitors. Such were Jacques Copeau, Charles Vildrac, a tiny and charming painter called Doucet (later killed in the War) Auguste Bréal and others. When we went for jaunts to Paris with him he took us to see various painters, among them Picasso then quite young and little known, Matisse, and even to rather stiff and alarming luncheon parties with a dealer like Vollard, made worth while by the Cézannes and Renoirs mysteriously produced from cellars . . .

. . . In 1911 Virginia and Adrian decided to give up the house in Fitzroy Square and move to a large house in Brunswick Square which they proposed to share with friends of whom Leonard Woolf was one . . . The other inhabitants, besides Leonard Woolf, were Maynard Keynes, Duncan Grant and Gerald Shove. This meant that Thursday evenings were given up, but members of Bloomsbury met as often or oftener than before. Brunswick Square was a little nearer Gordon Square than was Fitzroy Square and all sorts of parties at all hours of the day or night happened constantly. Rooms were decorated, people made to sit for their portraits, champagne was produced (rashly left unlocked up by Maynard Keynes who was half the time in Cambridge), to while away the morning sittings — all seemed a sizzle of excitement . . . Then (in 1912?) Leonard Woolf and Virginia were married and presently moved to another part of London and later to Richmond.

It was in these years, from 1909 or -10 to 1914 that there came the great expansion and

VANESSA STEPHEN PAINTING HER FIRST COMMISSIONED PORTRAIT (LADY ROBERT CECIL)
AT ASHEHAM, 1905

DUNCAN GRANT
TENNIS PLAYERS, 1912

development of Bloomsbury, that life seemed fullest of interest and promise and expansion of all kinds. Most of the members were writers or civil servants, only two in the earlier part of this time, Duncan Grant and myself, were painters. But when Roger Fry came bringing in his train painters both English and French the general attention was more directed to painting and less perhaps to the meaning of good. Other painters such as Sickert, Spencer Gore, F. Etchells, Henry Lamb and Francis Dodd, who were often in our company and on the friendliest terms with everyone, without belonging to Bloomsbury, helped to encourage talk about the visual arts. And then came the great excitement of the Post-Impressionist exhibition in 1910-11 which caused even more dismay and disapproval than Bloomsbury itself. How full of life those days seemed. Everything was brim full of interest and ideas and it certainly was for many of us 'very heaven' to be alive.

It must now be almost incredible how unaware we were of the disaster so soon to come. I do not know how much the politicians then foresaw, but I think that we in Bloomsbury had only the haziest ideas as to what was going on in the rest of Europe. How could we be interested in such matters when first getting to know well the great artists of the immediate past and those following them, when beauty was springing up under one's feet so vividly that violent abuse was hurled at it and genius considered to be insanity, when the writers were pricking up their ears and raising their voices lest too much attention should be given to painting: when music joined in the general chorus with sounds which excited ecstasy rage and derision:

a great new freedom seemed about to come and perhaps would have come, if it had not been for motives and ambitions of which we knew nothing. But surely such unawareness can never come again and it is difficult to explain it to those who cannot hope to feel it . . .

David Garnett, The Golden Echo, *1953*

. . . Adrian Stephen and his sister Virginia had recently moved to a lovely house in the middle of the north side of Brunswick Square and Adrian invited me to come round there to tea. As in most of the Brunswick Square houses, the big ground-floor dining-room had a round end and this room Adrian later on let to Maynard Keynes. Duncan Grant and his friend Frederick Etchells had painted its walls with a continuous London street scene, in which the centre of dramatic interest was a fallen cabhorse with the driver of the hansom still perched precariously aloft, though the cab was tilted forward with the shafts touching the pavement.

Adrian's friends met in the big drawing-room which stretched across the whole front of the house on the first floor. On its west wall, opposite the fireplace, was a huge painting executed by Duncan and Adrian working together, representing, in post-impressionist style, a mixed tennis doubles. One of the players, a female in the left foreground, was almost a triangle of yellow skirt, standing on one foot with the other one raised stiffly. In spite of the distortion and the violent colours, I liked it very much.

Besides these mural paintings there were several by Duncan standing around or even hanging on the walls, for he appeared to be almost an inmate of the house . . .

Vanessa Bell, Notes on Bloomsbury, *1951*

. . . Bloomsbury was not destroyed as probably many other circles were destroyed by the departure of all its young men to the wars. Perhaps one reason for much of the later abuse was that many were Conscientious Objectors. For some time therefore they were let alone and quietly pursued their usual professions. Women of course were not conscripted during that war and could do as they liked. So for a time Bloomsbury still existed even if crushed and bored by the outer world. The excitement and joy had gone. The hostility of the general public was real now, no longer a ridiculous and even stimulating joke, and the dreariness of the universal Khaki seemed only too appropriate. There was not even fear to create sympathy in unlikely quarters as in the last war. All the world was hostile close round one and Bloomsbury had no changing atmosphere in which to move and expand and grow. So when the young men were finally forced to take some share in what was going on for the most part they chose to work on farms, and this meant a dispersal and general scattering.

Most went to the country: but some like Maynard Keynes and others from Cambridge came to London to do war work. He took our house, 46 Gordon Square, and lived there with three or four others during the War, eventually continuing to live there for the rest of his life. I was among those who left London in 1916 and when I came back three years later I realized very clearly how all had changed. Nothing happens twice and Bloomsbury had had its day. It dissolved in the newer world . . .

POST - IMPRESSIONISM

MANET AND THE POST-IMPRESSIONISTS, THE EXHIBITION THAT ENRAGED A COMPLACENT PUBLIC WITH THE SHOCK OF THE NEW, OPENED IN THE GRAFTON GALLERIES IN LONDON IN NOVEMBER 1910.

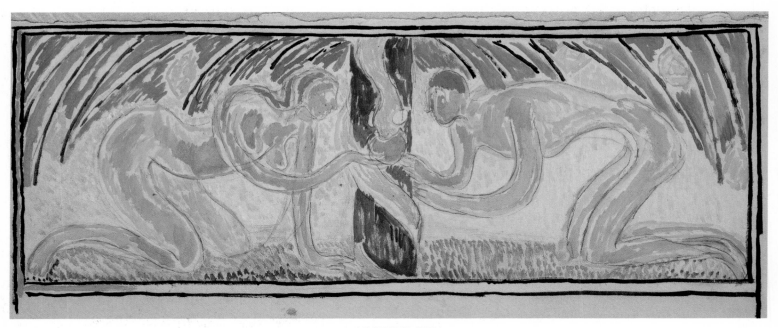

VANESSA BELL
ADAM AND EVE, 1913

Its impresario was Roger Fry, 'the newest and most learned of young critics', who had first met Vanessa Bell in 1904 and who had been absorbed into the Bloomsbury Group by 1910. Roger Fry, born in 1866, was more than ten years older than his Bloomsbury colleagues; his family were Quakers, and his father, Sir Edward Fry, a lawyer, was knighted on his appointment as Lord Justice of Appeal in 1877. Roger, his second son (there were also six sisters), was destined for a scientific career, and he went up to King's College, Cambridge, to read Natural Sciences in 1885 (the year of Duncan Grant's birth). He was elected to the Apostles, and graduated with a First Class degree.

References to Roger Fry's experiences in Cambridge are given in Part I, and their relevance is discussed in the Introduction. Fry's preoccupation with art and aesthetics, so alien to his family's concerns and values, was stimulated there. His decision to train as an artist when he left Cambridge was a brave one: his parents could not understand it, and he constantly considered himself a failure in their eyes. He embarked on his new career with the energy and enthusiasm that he devoted to all his activities, and his struggles with the art as well with the history and meaning of painting were intensified by his travels on the Continent. His descriptions of architecture and landscape as well as of painting and sculpture reveal the vivacity of his responses. At the same time, however, it was not enough to look, one had to analyse the significance of every detail before one could begin to understand, and classify the overall achievement. He was involved in these intensive studies of early Italian artists in 1894, when he went to Florence with A.M. Daniel (see page 52), and he probably met Bernard Berenson at some time during the 1890s. These encounters with connoisseurship, and with the role of the *Kunstforscher*, obviously led to his American experience, his struggles with J. Pierpont Morgan, and his brief time as Curator of the Department of Paintings at the Metropolitan Museum in New York.

This potential expansion in his career had coincided with his marriage in 1896 to Helen Coombe, a young artist associated with A.H. Mackmurdo's Century Guild. Two years later Helen suffered from the first of her devastating attacks of mental illness. Fry's letters reveal his distress, his dwindling hopes for a cure (she had brief periods of recovery), and his constant need for money to support her and their two children. He had published his first book *Giovanni Bellini* in 1899, and he contributed his first article *Giotto and His Time* to the *Monthly Review* in 1901 (see page 53). He also became a regular contributor to the influential *Burlington Magazine*, and was in growing demand as a lecturer. In 1909 (while he was still working for the Metropolitan Museum) he built his house, Durbins, at Guildford, and as well as continuing, with some frustration, his own career as a painter, he was also involved with the activities of the New English Art Club.

In spite of his reputation as a connoisseur and a specialist in Italian painting, Fry was obviously aware of contemporary developments, so that although his championship of modern French art in 1910 and his apotheosis of Cézanne has all the appearances of a revelation, it was (as is explained in the Introduction) the culmination of his preoccupation with an aesthetic ideal that was to have certain links with Bloomsbury theory. Fry's discovery of the significance of form enabled him to re-evaluate his ideas about the nature of content. Content could now be divorced from narrative and the need to represent or symbolize appearances, and become an end in itself. For Fry, in 1910, 'art had begun to recover once more the language of design', and the exhibitions of 1910 and 1912 were organized to demonstrate and explain these ideas to an uncomprehending and mostly hostile public.

Roger Fry: the newest and most learned of young critics

Roger Fry to G. L. Dickinson   *Roma, 15 February 1891*

Rome at last after many accidental delays ... You are decidedly wrong about St Peter's. Of course it doesn't impress one like a great Christian Cathedral but it is the most perfect expression of the Christianity of Borgias and della Roveres that one could conceive. It is splendidly mundane — untinged by any religious or altruistic emotion — all based on power and wealth and the intellect that could scramble best for them. It may wear off, but my first impression is that almost everything except the west front is very first-rate. The simplicity to which all the architectural forms are reduced could only be due to the influence of a mind as great as Michelangelo's, and the mere fact that the place is overlaid with bombastic tasteless statuary doesn't touch the grandeur and really Classical reserve of the whole. Oh that I could send you some of the sunlight of this divine city of splashing fountains and sunburnt domes; it is a revelation of what climate can do. Yes, Italy is much better than I ever thought, but it smells much worse...

Firenze, 21 April 1891

... I wish you wouldn't say such things about the NEAC [New English Art Club] ... Probably you can't see form in a picture unless it has an edge to it, while in reality it consists of true relief and I would bet there is more form in a pictorial sense in the NEAC than in most exhibitions. Forgive this serious jaw, but I'm sure you've not got hold of quite the right way of looking at these things...

Florence is splendid, in some ways the jolliest thing I've had yet, but I get rather sick of these attitudinizing saints with their heads cut open or their entrails coming out. I've come round now about Andrea del Sarto, he's another of the Italians who can only be judged rightly by fresco, being entirely absorbed in the delight of contour and having no interest in appearances in general, like the Venetians. The Lorenzo Library and the Chapel of the Medici make me quite certain that Michelangelo was much the greatest architect that has lived since Greek times; it is a perfectly new effect produced by the most subtle arrangement in proportion, and expresses an idea at least as complete and intelligible as a sonata of Beethoven's, which indeed it much resembles.

Botticelli's *Primavera* is as splendid as I had expected and renews all the delight I had when I first saw your photo and which I feared I should never get again out of Pre-Raphaelite painting.

Virginia Woolf, Roger Fry, A Biography, 1940

The process of digestion had now to begin. It was difficult; he had swallowed so much. He had seen enough in those few months to make him sure that compromise was impossible — his life's work was to lie not in laboratories, but among pictures. He had only taken a rapid glance at Raphael, Michaelangelo and the rest, but he guessed that the mass behind them was prodigious, and that it would need a lifetime to take its measure. But there was also the other desire — the desire to paint himself...

Naturally the few months that he spent in London with his family on his return were gloomy. 'I am very sick about things in general just now and cannot manage to work properly', he wrote. After Italy, Bayswater was less tolerable than ever. The Quaker atmosphere, he said, made him 'into a strange jelly-like mass with about as much consciousness as a chloroformed amoeba'. And after Italy the atmosphere of Applegarth Studios, Hammersmith, with Francis Bate to instruct and Briton Revière to advise was a little elementary. The solution seemed to be a second foreign tour, this time to France, to continue his education at the headquarters of art, the Académie Julian at Paris. He went there in 1892.

Roger Fry to Lady Fry   *Paris, 29 January 1892*

... I have been spending all my time going about seeing buildings and pictures so far, and am immensely struck with the high level of modern Paris architecture. Most of Napoleon III's work on the Louvre seems to me equal to the best work of the Renaissance in detail as well as general design, and that was done at a time when we were producing our most horrible buildings. But everywhere one finds really beautiful houses and always in a severe and tasteful style depending on proportion and fitness of the parts ...

Roger Fry to Nathaniel Wedd   *Paris, 21 February 1892*

The work in the studios isn't anything so very wonderful; in fact, the average is quite low, but there are some very clever men, and the caricatures on the walls are wonderfully brilliant and naturally indecent, for they're a swinish set. But there is so large a preponderance of Americans that I've not had much to do with French students ... The Luxembourg is disappointing; only about six really first-rate things I think and an awful lot of second-rate stuff; the sculpture, perhaps partly because I know less about it, seems to be on a much higher level. They have developed a distinctly French type which is not Classical or Renaissance or Medieval and yet not mere realism either. I think one of the most striking things about Paris is that so much of the best art is used on public works — and not hidden away in private collections. These French people have a much keener national consciousness than we have, which makes one inclined to forgive their arrogance and vanity. Paris is first of all the capital of France and after that a place for people to live and amuse themselves in ...

Virginia Woolf, Roger Fry, A Biography, 1940

... Yet France was to mean more to Roger Fry than any other country. It was to mean something different. Italy, as the skipping summary of the letters is enough to show, was a lovely land of brilliant light and clear outlines; it was a place where one worked hard all day seeing Old Masters; where one settled down at night in some little pub to sample strange dishes and to argue with other English travellers about art. But it was not a place with a living art and a living civilization that one could share with the Italians themselves. France was to be that country. He was to spend his happiest days there, he was to find his greatest inspiration as a critic there ...

PART II

Roger Fry to Sir Edward Fry   *Chelsea, 23 November 1893*

. . . Of course I am much annoyed about the NEAC especially as I think so far as I can be impartial to my own work that it was quite worthy a place in the exhibition, an opinion which is shared by Mr Bate and others whom I have asked. Of course I shall be sorry if I find that it is impossible to exhibit there, because I still think it the best place to exhibit in England . . .

Roger Fry to Margery Fry   *Firenze* [1894]

. . . We work five or six hours a day in the galleries and Daniel [A. M. Daniel, later Director of the National Gallery], who is very learned, helps me to do the thing more thoroughly than I otherwise should, and his keenness in tracing out hardly known artists and comparing their works and tracing their development is immense. I've never got such a grip of early art before, never learned to distinguish so much between the individualities of similar painters . . .

Roger Fry to R. C. Trevelyan   *Chelsea, 15 March 1896*

. . . I fence with Hubert Crackanthorpe, who has come to live near here and whose house I have decorated with infinite care. Alas! he has proceeded to furnish it and therewith to destroy all my schemes of colour or at all events to mar them; fancy hanging photographs in a room where I had given him white walls and black wood dados. Oh, the pity of it . . .

Roger Fry to Helen Coombe   *Friday night* [1896]

I'm afraid you'll have to love me after all because I want you to so very much — does that reasoning seem inadequate; perhaps it is — and the thing looks impossible. You to whom style is everything and me who can only appreciate style all the more because I haven't got it. You who live in appearance and care nothing about the *whyness* of the *what*, to whom the what is sufficient — I who am always grubbing in the entrails of things to find out their causes, I who believe in reality, you who don't. Yes, all that makes it very difficult but not impossible; that is all I can console myself with. But I have vowed that I am going to try not to be other than quite my natural self with you at whatever cost and however much I feel the inferiority because I don't think it's fair on you — though I believe you are cute enough to get at the real me through all disguises. Besides I'm a damned bad actor . . .

Roger Fry to R. C. Trevelyan   *Chelsea, Sunday* [Autumn 1896]

I've had rather an awful time with my people. I'm so awfully sorry for my father and his disappointment in me that I made a huge effort to get through the misunderstandings between us and be quite frank. It was a mistake and only pained him and my mother; I suppose it is quite impossible for the two generations to meet even with

tremendous goodwill and great self-restraint on both sides. Only it has made me awfully depressed and I could hardly pull myself together for the lectures — it happened just before them. However they went off well enough. I think they are much the best I've done . . .

Helen's harpsichord is going to be a great success, at least I think so. I am in these things absolutely impartial and objective so you may take my word for it: it is damned good . . .

Roger Fry to Sir Edward Fry   *9 Savoy Mansions, 13 June* 1898

. . . I cannot even now realize what it would mean to me to lose Helen — she has given me a new sense of confidence and hopefulness in life and we have both of us enjoyed such happiness, as, I think, we neither knew before, and which has increased continually and far beyond what I had ever dared to hope for. But I know quite well that if only she is spared, our sufferings will only make us more dear to one another. I cannot help hoping now that this will be so, but still even now the doctors dare not say anything too definite. Please give Mother my dear love . . .

Virginia Woolf, Roger Fry, A Biography, *1940*

. . . To write of Roger Fry as he was before his wife's illness is to write of someone who differed fundamentally from the man whom his friends knew later. He was never again to know perfect freedom from anxiety; the 'beauty of life as a whole' was shattered, and the centre upon which he depended was shaken. The first shock was followed by the torture of prolonged illness. Death, which then seemed to him the most terrible possibility, was averted. But there were harassing alternations of hope and despair . . .

Roger Fry to Nathaniel Wedd   9 June 1899

What makes ART so dangerous, I think, is that it has got separated from religion and life; by religion it could hang on to life, without it it can't, and so one has to make it a religion by itself, to the great detriment of both or rather of all three . . .

Roger Fry, 'Giotto and His Time' in Monthly Review, *1901 (reprinted in* Vision and Design, *1920)*

. . . It is difficult to avoid the temptation to say of Giotto that he was the greatest artist that ever lived, a phrase which has been used of too many masters to retain its full emphasis. But at least he was the most prodigious phenomenon in the known history of art. Starting with little but the crude realism of Cimabue, tempered by the effete accomplishment of the Byzantines*, to have created an art capable of expressing the whole range of human emotions; to have found, almost without a guide, how to treat the raw material of life itself in a style so direct, so pliant to the idea, and yet so essentially grandiose and heroic; to have guessed intuitively almost all the principles of representation which it required nearly two centuries of enthusiastic research to establish scientifically — to have accomplished all this is surely a more astounding performance than any other one artist has ever achieved.

But the fascination Giotto's art exercises is due in part to his position in the development of modern culture. Coming at the same time as Dante, he shares with him the privilege of seeing life as a single, self-consistent, and systematic whole. It was a moment of equilibrium between the conflicting tendencies of human activity, a moment when such men as Dante and Giotto could exercise to their full their critical and analytical powers without destroying the unity of a cosmic theory based on theology . . .

* This passage now seems to me to underestimate the work of Giotto's predecessors with which we are now much better acquainted (1920).

Vanessa Bell, Memories of Roger Fry, *October 1934*

There is always a certain fascination in recalling the first time one saw anyone who later became one's friend, and it is strange how frequently it is possible to do so, though probably at the time one was unaware of anything but the casual meeting with a stranger. How clearly after more than 30 years, for I suppose it was about the year 1902 or 3, do I remember one summer afternoon in the Fellow's Garden at Kings [College Cambridge] seeing across the lawn two tall figures walking together, the woman perhaps taller than the man and certainly looking so in her long straight dress. 'Those are the Roger Fry's' said Walter Headlam. I knew his name already as a lecturer on Italian art and perhaps that is why I remember the scene so clearly. But, hating lectures, I had never been to hear him, though he lectured very near us, I think in the small lecture hall attached to the Albert Hall and on a subject which must have interested me — also I had heard of him as the newest and most learned of young critics — but for some reason I did not go. So it was at Cambridge that I first saw him and that one vision is all I have of those days for we did not speak . . .

Roger Fry to Helen Fry   *Vicenza, Tuesday, Autumn 1902*

. . . I was determined this time to see Mantua so I got up at five thirty and managed to get there by eight in pouring rain. I just managed to see everything, get back to Verona, see a church there and catch the train on here in time for dinner; a pretty full day. Mantua is a place we must stay at . . . The Gonzaga Palace is incredible; one wanders on through suites of immense halls covered with stucco friezes and gigantic caryatids and carved gilt ceilings all literally tumbling to pieces. Then there's the Mantegna room. It's quite different to what I had imagined. It's the most lovely colour and so fresh and gay for Mantegna, whites and tender sweet blues with a few pale reds and cold greens and rather purplish-grey flesh — marvellous. Really about the best wall decoration I know. It's a little hard after that to see Giulio Romano at the Palazzo del Té, but even he managed sometimes to decorate finely in a Pompeian style and his architecture is splendid . . .

Vanessa Bell, Memories of Roger Fry, *October 1934*

. . . I think the next time [Vanessa met Roger Fry] must have been at dinner at Desmond's [MacCarthy], certainly it was after my father's death in 1904. Desmond was living with his mother in Chelsea and asked me to dinner and I feeling very nervous and shy found myself sitting next to Roger Fry. He was vaguely associated in my mind with other

terrifying figures of about the same age, all connected more or less with what then seemed the most go ahead group in modern art, the New English Art Club. I knew Charles Furse, then lately dead and had found him formidable and crushing. Slightly less so perhaps than Tonks who had taught or rather squashed me at the Slade. In fact all members of the NEAC seemed somehow to have the secret of the art universe within their grasp, a secret one was not worthy to learn, especially if one was that terrible low creature, a female painter. 'He's another of them' I thought and prepared to be silent and afraid. But somehow I wasn't — I must have ventured some remark and found it listened to and understood and felt encouraged to continue . . . I remember Helen Fry there too, looking melancholy and quiet and rather ill, in a dress which Roger told me he had designed and which I hastily criticized but only to myself, as 'arty'. She or Roger asked me to go and see them at Hampstead . . .

The visit to Hampstead did not happen at once — I think Helen Fry must have been ill and perhaps they went away — various things prevented it, but at last I went. It was in the summer I think. I know that I walked into a long room with windows opening to a garden at the back. Both Roger and Helen were there and both seemed glad I had come. The children came in, tiny creatures of about 2 and 3, Julian like Roger with lovely dark eyes — Helen seemed again ill and worried, but friendly to me. She had, Roger told me years later, taken a liking to me and I felt vaguely sorry for her. She seemed ill at ease and rather forlorn though Roger I think was aware of her at every instant. He told me of some early painting he had been to see that day — how *did* one see such things in London I wondered to myself, the whole world of dealers was unknown to me. But though the scene is clear to me I cannot remember what we talked of — only the general impression remains of a strange alive household, not altogether happy but with a tremendous force and interest of some kind at work in it. I never went there again. My own life was completely upset and when I saw them again I was married myself . . .

Roger Fry to Lady Fry   *Hampstead, 18 April* 1903
         . . . I must share at once with you the good news about my show [Roger Fry's first exhibition, at the Carfax Gallery, London]. Today was private view day and they wired to me that they have sold thirteen things, eleven water-colours and two oils, for a total of £106 . . .

Situations complex and strange

Roger Fry to Helen Fry   *New York, Tuesday 10 January* 1905
         This is business. Just heard offer. Head of [Metropolitan] Museum to be Sir Purdon Clarke — he will be more or less of a figurehead. I am offered the second place with reversion of headship if I succeed. I to have £1,600 a year, travelling expenses in Europe for 6 months in the year and to be allowed to write and lecture, which should bring in a good lot. Well, I shall see Morgan [James Pierpont Morgan — banker, art collector and

entrepreneur] tomorrow; I am going to Washington to dine with him and the President of the USA. It's alarming and interesting. I shall talk over details with him and we shall see what comes of it . . .

There are heaps of really nice interesting people here and the intellectual society is very friendly and accessible, and altogether I think it's better than going on being blocked and crabbed and buffeted at home. I am really inclined to accept . . .

Roger Fry to Sir Edward Fry   *City Club of NY, 2 March* 1906

. . . Morgan has as usual been obstreperous: tried to get out of any new arrangement. I believe it will all be settled, but I have had to send a kind of ultimatum to [William] Laffan saying that Morgan must accept my letter (the one you drew up) as final or else I shall resign. If I resign I shall, I hope, have the National Gallery [in London] but even without that anything would be better than being at his mercy . . . The situations are all very complex and strange, and the intrigues and jealousies make society here almost chaotic. Moreover, everyone seems very nervous about public opinion and very few seem to have any courage. I sat next to Mark Twain the other night at dinner and found him a really fine, generous and liberal-minded gentleman, altogether one of the fine men — and he has the courage to speak out for what is honest and humane. I sometimes wonder whether this society isn't drifting back to sheer barbarism . . .

Virginia Woolf, Roger Fry, A Biography, *1940*

. . . But general reflections upon America were always being interrupted by doubts as to his own position. That was becoming more and more precarious. It was partly his own fault — he could not conceal his opinions. 'The one criticism of myself that comes back to me in roundabout ways is that I have not yet learned not to say what I think', he wrote home. 'But I'm not in a hurry to mend it.' He said what he thought, even when it was the opposite of what the President [Morgan] thought. And the President was omnipotent. To Roger Fry's amazement, no one dared withstand him. Therefore, 'one never knows what turn things at the Museum may take'. But the best account of his peculiar relationship is given in a description that Roger Fry wrote many years later of a journey that he made with Pierpont Morgan in 1907. There was an exhibition at Perugia, and Morgan summoned his adviser to consider possible purchases for the Museum . . .

'. . . The party descended and passed through the hall, eyed with awestruck admiration by the expectant Italian counts, the Levantine Jews and all the other human flotsam that was drawn into the whirlpool of Morgan's wealth. They indeed but most of all the Italians looked at Morgan with something like worship. His wealth affected them not merely as something from which they might hope for doles but as something glorious and romantic in itself. Their passion was so great as to be almost disinterested. The mere thought that one man had so much wealth seemed to them ennobling and uplifting and incredibly more romantic than royalty itself. . .

It was a beautiful day and we were spinning along the road to Assisi. For a wonder Mr

Morgan was in a good humour, he didn't know how bored he was going to be with the frescoes at Assisi where moreover there was nothing one could buy. . .

ROGER FRY

The motor spun along driven by a horribly skilful but reckless Italian chauffeur who had his ideas of how an ultra-royal and Morganatic car should be driven, namely to cause as much terror to the inhabitants as possible. Oxen dragging loads of hay plunged wildly into ditches and up the opposite bank, fowls, dogs and children rushed screaming away and everyone realized that Morgan was a real millionaire. So we spun along until a particularly deep canniveau gave the car such a jerk that Morgan was projected violently up to the ceiling and his hat crushed down over his eyes. (He wore a kind of truncated top-hat). Then there was an apoplectic splutter of rage, the Cavaliere was called from the front seat, the driver warned, and the car driven less impressively. Assisi was a failure. Mr Morgan was displeased with the condition of the frescoes...

Such was our triumphal progress through Italy. At Siena the whole of the wooden floor of the Cathedral was taken up that il Morgan might see the Mosaics. The Queen of Italy had visited Siena a little before and had asked in vain for this...'

The modern vision

Roger Fry to the Editor of The Burlington Magazine   [March 1908]

... Impressionism accepts the totality of appearances and shows how to render that; but thus to say everything amounts to saying nothing — there is left no power to express the personal attitude and emotional conviction. The organs of expression — line, mass, colour — have become so fused together, so lost in the flux of appearance, that they cease to deliver any intelligible message, and the next step that is taken must be to re-assert these. The first thing the neo-Impressionist must do is to recover the long obliterated contour and to fill it with simple undifferentiated masses.

I should like to consider in this light some of the most characteristic painters of this movement. Of these M. Signac is the only one to whom the title neo-Impressionist properly applies. Here is a man feeling in a vague, unconscious way a dissatisfaction at the total licence of Impressionism and he deliberately invents for himself a restraining formula — that of rectangular blobs of paint. He puts himself deliberately where more fortunate circumstances placed the mosaic artist, and then lets himself go as far in the direction of realistic Impressionism as his formula will allow. I do not defend this, in spite of the subtle powers of observation and the ingenuity which M. Signac displays, because I do not think it is ever worth-while to imitate in one medium the effects of another, but his case is interesting as a tribute to the need of the artist to recover some constraint: to escape, at whatever cost, from the anarchic licence of Impressionism.

Two other artists, MM. Cézanne and Paul Gauguin, are not really Impressionists at all. They are proto-Byzantines rather than neo-Impressionists. They have already attained to the contour, and assert its value with keen emphasis. They fill the contour with wilfully simplified and unmodulated masses, and rely for their whole effect upon a well-considered co-ordination of the simplest elements. There is no need for me to praise Cézanne — his position is already assured — but if one compares his still-life in the International [Society] Exhibition with Monet's, I think it will be admitted that it marks a great advance in intellectual content. It leaves far less to the casual dictation of natural appearance. The relations of every tone and colour are deliberately chosen and stated in unmistakable terms. In the placing of objects, in the relation of one form to another, in the values of colour which indicate mass, and in the purely decorative elements of design, Cézanne's work seems to me to betray a finer, more scrupulous artistic sense.

In Gauguin's work you admit that 'some trace of design and some feeling for the decorative arrangement of colour may still be found', but I cannot think that the author of so severely grandiose, so strict a design as the Femmes Maories or of so splendidly symbolic a decoration as the Te Arti Vahiné deserves the fate of so contemptuous a recognition. Here is an artist of striking talent who, in spite of occasional boutades, has seriously set himself to rediscover some of the essential elements of design without throwing away what his immediate predecessors had taught him. . .

Roger Fry, Retrospect, *1920* (Vision and Design)

. . . I think I can claim that my study of the Old Masters was never much tainted by archaeological curiosity. I tried to study them in the same spirit as I might study contemporary artists, and I always regretted that there was no modern art capable of satisfying my predilections. I say there was no modern art because none such was known to me, but all the time there was one who had already worked out the problem which seemed to me insoluble of how to use the modern vision with the constructive design of the older masters. By some extraordinary ill luck I managed to miss seeing Cézanne's work till some considerable time after his death. I had heard of him vaguely from time to time as a kind of hidden oracle of ultra-impressionism, and, in consequence, I expected to find myself entirely unreceptive to his art. To my intense surprise I found myself deeply moved . . .

Roger Fry, An Essay in Aesthetics, 1909 (Vision and Design)

. . . Morality, then, appreciates emotion by the standard of resultant action. Art appreciates emotion in and for itself . . .

. . . We must therefore give up the attempt to judge the work of art by its reaction on life, and consider it as an expression of emotions regarded as ends in themselves. And this brings us back to the idea we had already arrived at, of art as the expression of the imaginative life.

If, then, an object of any kind is created by man not for use, for its fitness to actual life, but as an object of art, an object subserving the imaginative life, what will its qualities be? It must in the first place be adapted to that disinterested intensity of contemplation, which we have found to be the effect of cutting off the responsive action. It must be suited to that heightened power of perception which we found to result therefrom . . .

. . . One chief aspect of order in a work of art is unity; unity of some kind is necessary for our restful contemplation of the work of art as a whole, since if it lacks unity we cannot contemplate it in its entirety, but we shall pass outside it to other things necessary to complete its unity.

In a picture this unity is due to a balancing of the attractions of the eye about the central line of the picture. The result of this balance of attractions is that the eye rests willingly within the bounds of the picture. Dr Denman Ross of Harvard University has made a most valuable study of the elementary considerations upon which this balance is based in his

'Theory of Pure Design'. He sums up his results in the formula that a composition is of value in proportion to the number of orderly connections which it displays . . .

. . . When the artist passes from pure sensations to emotions aroused by means of sensations, he uses natural forms which, in themselves, are calculated to move our emotions, and he presents these in such a manner that the forms themselves generate in us emotional states, based upon the fundamental necessities of our physical and physiological nature . . .

We may, then, dispense once for all with the idea of likeness to Nature, of correctness or incorrectness as a test, and consider only whether the emotional elements inherent in natural form are adequately discovered, unless, indeed, the emotional idea depends at any point upon likeness, or completeness of representation.

Roger Fry to Sir Edward Fry   *Durbins, 14 February* 1910

The blow I expected has fallen. Morgan could not forgive me for trying to get that picture [*Virgin and Child*, attributed to Fra Angelico; Morgan had reserved it for himself] for the Museum . . .

I send you copies of the letters I have received and of my reply. It is useless to make any fuss about it. I could get no satisfaction from these people, but they have behaved vilely . . .

Durbins and Bloomsbury

Roger Fry, A Possible Domestic Architecture, *1918*

. . . The house which I planned and built for myself was the result of certain particular needs and habits . . . I required a house of a certain size for my family within easy reach of London. I looked at a great many houses and found that those which had a sufficient number of rooms were all gentlemen's establishments, with lodge, stabling, and greenhouses. Now it was characteristic of my purse that I could not afford to keep up a gentleman's establishment and of my tastes that I could not endure to. I was a town dweller, and I wanted a town house and a little garden in the country. As I could not find what I wanted, the idea came into my head that I must build it or go without. The means at my disposal were definitely limited; the question was therefore whether I could build a house of the required size with that sum. I made a plan containing the number of rooms of the sizes I required, and got an estimate. It was largely in excess of the sum I possessed for the purpose. I feared I must give up my scheme when I met a friend who had experimented in building cheap cottages on his estate, and learned from him that the secret of economy was concentration of plan. I also discovered in discussing my first estimate that roofs were cheaper than walls. I thereupon started on a quite different plan, in which I arranged the rooms to form as nearly as possible a solid block, and placed a number of the rooms in a hipped or Mansard roof. It will be seen that, so far, the planning of the house was merely the discovery of a possible equation between my needs and the sum at my disposal . . .

I hate Elizabethan rooms with their low ceilings in spite of their prettiness, and I love the interiors of the baroque palaces of Italy — I determined to have one room of generous dimensions and particularly of great height . . .

The estimate for this new concentrated plan, in spite of the large dimensions of the living place, came to little more than half the estimate for the former plan, and made my project feasible, provided that I could calculate all details and did not run into extras.

So far then there has been no question of architecture; it has been merely solving the problem of personal needs and habits, and of costs, and if architecture there is to be, it should, I think, come directly out of the solution of these problems . . . The artistic or architectural part of this house was confined, then, merely to the careful choice of proportions within certain fixed limits defined by needs, and neither time, money, nor thought was expended on giving the house the appearance of any particular style . . .

Vanessa Bell, Memories of Roger Fry, *1934*

. . . It was again at Cambridge that I next met Roger. Clive and I had been spending a week there, I think early in 1908, and on that long platform waiting for the Monday morning train I said 'There's Roger Fry — but I don't think he remembers me'. We went up to him, however, and whether he remembered me or not, a question we disputed later, I introduced Clive and we entered the same carriage. He had brought a MS of course and intended to write an article or lecture on the way to London. But talk began and continued unceasingly. As he sate opposite me in the corner I looked at his face bent a little down towards his MS but not reading, considering, listening, waiting to reply, intensely alive but quiet. 'What astonishing beauty', I thought, looking at the austere modelling in the flat bright side-lights from the train windows. I do not think I talked much but he was becoming a real person to me, and it was suggested that we should go and see him at Guildford.

That first attempted visit I can more or less date because it was some time in the early Spring, before Quentin was born, in 1910. We went on a Sunday intending to lunch with him and arrived at Guildford only to find that no one at the empty Sunday station knew where Durbins was . . . We walked and walked, it seemed for many miles, but I was even less inclined to walk than I am normally, and at last gave it up in despair. We went back to Guildford, to the inn there, and ordered lunch and then sat down to wait for a train back to London and to write a letter explaining our absence. Clive was very cross and I was very tired, and I think that letter might have nipped a promising friendship in the bud. But some instinct interfered — some word was put in to show that complaints needn't be taken too seriously . . . However Roger took all the blame on himself for not meeting us at the station and we were begged to come again when everything should be perfectly arranged. So we went, only a week or two later I think . . . [the house] was very bare with a new garden in terraces running down to the road and no trees except a row of baby poplars. It was built on the side of a hill and faced south and seems to me in memory to have been nearly always filled with blazing sunshine. Every inch of house and garden were exposed to the sun. The great shutters tried to keep it out but not with complete success. The floors were bare polished wood with rugs, the walls were pale greys and full greens, the doors and all the wood a smoky brown, unpainted. I came to think the house perhaps one of Roger's most successful works, for everywhere it depended upon a most carefully balanced proportion, but there was a certain bareness and austerity to which one had to get accustomed. The only room which could by any possibility be called cosy was Roger's own studio or study rather, for it was far too full of books and sunlight to be a studio, and there one could with comfortable chairs, a peat fire and central heating, get up a good fug and satisfy one's lower instincts. But the large hall, used by everyone as a drawing room, passage, sitting room with its three long windows, was perhaps beautiful but hardly comfortable . . . Helen Fry was there . . . Then I saw what the tragedy was in this household, for the poor creature sat silent, utterly miserable and aloof. One could not tell how much she understood, but it was clearly impossible to talk to her. She murmured sometimes vaguely to herself and Roger left her out of the conversation so that one could not but do likewise. After lunch we went for a walk rather to my dismay, but Roger of course had noticed no reason why I should not jump over the moon and I stumbled along in my long loose dress doing my best to keep up for one could not miss the talk. Coming back I found myself alone with Roger and Helen and as we reached the road leading up to Durbins she stopped, murmured something about the children and wandered off. Rather to my surprise Roger let her go — then said to me, 'She thinks she hears the children, but it's no use, they're away.' Helen gave up her search and followed us to the house. She took me up to her room then, which was the most natural thing she had done and asked me if I were tired. For she I think had seen what no man ever sees, that I was going to have a child. She looked so utterly miserable standing there that I nearly put my arms round her and asked if I couldn't help, but I was too shy, the moment went and we came down. I have never seen her since . . .

The Post-Impressionist Exhibitions

Roger Fry, Retrospect, *1920* (Vision and Design)

     . . . In the next few years I became increasingly interested in the art of Cézanne and of those like Gauguin and van Gogh who at that time represented the first effects of his profound influence on modern art, and I gradually recognized that what I had hoped for as a possible event of some future century had already occurred, that art had begun to recover once more the language of design and to explore its so long neglected possibilities. Thus it happened that when at the end of 1911, by a curious series of chances, I was in a position to organize an exhibition at the Grafton Galleries, I seized the opportunity to bring before the English public a selection of works conforming to the new direction. For purposes of convenience it was necessary to give these artists a name, and I chose, as being the vaguest and most non-committal, the name of Post-Impressionist . . .

Desmond MacCarthy, Memories, *1953*

     . . . What was the exhibition to be called? That was the next question. Roger and I and a young journalist who was to help us with publicity, met to consider this: and it was at that meeting that a word which is now safely embedded in the English language — 'post-impressionism' — was invented. Roger first suggested various terms like 'expressionism', which aimed at distinguishing these artists from the impressionists; but the journalist

wouldn't have that or any other of his alternatives. At last Roger, losing patience, said: 'Oh, let's just call them post-impressionists; at any rate, they came after the impressionists.' Later he handed over to me, with a few notes, the ticklish job of writing the preface to the catalogue

POSTER, 1912

— the unsigned preface. This work of mine was far more widely quoted than anything I was ever destined to write, and phrases from it like 'A good rocking-horse is more like a horse than the snapshot of a Derby winner' were quoted and re-quoted with laughter . . .

Presently we actually began to sell pictures. The Art Gallery at Helsinki bought a very fine Cézanne for £800, I remember; and when we closed, my share of the profits amounted to — what do you think? — over £460 — such a lump sum as I had never earned before, and would never earn again! Not only had the exhibition been the theme of non-stop correspondence in the papers and of pamphlet wars — all the best-known painters were, alas, against us — but it also provoked lectures from mental specialists. Fry himself did not make one penny out of the exhibition, nor did he out of the Omega workshops, which he started seven years later. Indeed, by introducing the works of Cézanne, Matisse, Seurat, Van Gogh, Gauguin and

Picasso to the British public, he smashed for a long time his reputation as an art critic. Kind people called him mad, and reminded others that his wife was in an asylum. The majority declared him to be a subverter of morals and art, and a blatant self-advertiser . . .

Vanessa Bell, Memories of Roger Fry, 1934

. . . How can one possibly describe the effect of that first Post Impressionist exhibition on English painters at that time? I knew very few of them and those few were none too good at expressing what they felt. The New English [Art Club] . . . was the most alive of existing institutions. Sickert and the Camden Town Group were producing work that was sympathetic, but for the most part rather timid — Sickert's own work of course always had life and character as well as exquisite taste and colour, but his followers too often seemed to have only taste. [Augustus] John was the rising genius and at one moment seemed to promise something strangely new and exciting. But that did not last — London knew little of Paris, incredibly little it seems now, and English painters were on the whole still under the Victorian cloud, either conscientiously painting effects of light, or trying to be poets or neo-Pre-Raphaelites . . . Exhibitions were far fewer then than they are now, and except I think for the tiny Carfax Gallery there was no dealer showing work by younger living painters such as are to be found by the dozen in Bond St. and St James's. The New Gallery to be sure sometimes had modern French paintings and it was there I first saw a work by Cézanne . . . I think paintings by Degas were also to be seen there, and I remember a very lovely little Van Gogh of flowers in a jug. Also there had been much earlier a show at some obscure gallery, I do not know which, of French Impressionists — some Manets and I think Pissarros, which left one wanting to see more . . . [realizing] that after all living painters might be as alive as the dead and that there was something besides the lovely quality of old paint to be aimed at, something fundamental and permanent and as discoverable now as in any other age. But above one were the professors saying 'Draw for seven years — learn anatomy and chemistry and the use of the stump . . .

Then, suddenly, bewilderingly, here, well arranged, not too many yet enough, in a pleasant gallery in Grafton St were all the painters one had had glimpses of. Cézanne, Van Gogh, Gauguin . . . The fuming and storming of the elders added to the fun of course, but in that first show the only possible shocking quality was that of unfamiliarity . . . here was a sudden pointing to a possible path, a sudden liberation and encouragement to feel for oneself which were absolutely overwhelming. Perhaps no one but a painter can understand it, and perhaps no one but a painter of a certain age. But it was as if at last one might say things one had always felt instead of trying to say things that other people told one to feel . . .

As far as any event of the kind can be said to be due to the courage and perception of one man that was certainly due to Roger Fry's. Probably he could have had no idea himself how tremendous an excitement he was preparing for painters. But the result was as exciting to himself as to anyone else.

Such was the excitement in London, so great were the crowds who came to abuse and mock and demand explanations if not apologies from the producer of all this excitement that it was almost impossible for ordinary lovers of painting to see the pictures in his company. Still once

or twice I did manage to do so — I remember those times very clearly, but of course the experience of seeing pictures with him, which was to be mine so often, cannot be described as it was then. Later impressions have no doubt got added to one's recollections. I think I was uneasy at first, distrustful no doubt of my own taste and afraid to give myself away. All the same that cannot have lasted long — for though I did not agree with much of what I understood to be his theories then . . . I found it easy to listen and to talk to someone whose feelings about the actual works were so largely in agreement with one's own . . .

Roger Fry, Preface to the Catalogue of the Second Post-Impressionist Exhibition, Grafton Galleries, 1912
THE FRENCH POST-IMPRESSIONISTS

When the first Post-Impressionist Exhibition was held in these Galleries two years ago the English public became for the first time fully aware of the existence of a new movement in art, a movement which was the more disconcerting in that it was no mere variation upon accepted themes but implied a reconsideration of the very purpose and aim as well as the methods of pictorial and plastic art. It was not surprising, therefore, that a public which had come to admire above everything in a picture the skill with which the artist produced illusion should have resented an art in which such skill was completely subordinated to the direct expression of feeling . . . The difficulty springs from a deep-rooted conviction, due to long-established custom, that the aim of painting is the descriptive imitation of natural forms. Now, these artists do not seek to give what can, after all, be but a pale reflex of actual appearance, but to arouse the conviction of a new and definite reality. They do not seek to imitate form, but to create form; not to imitate life, but to find an equivalent for life . . . In fact, they aim not at illusion but at reality.

The logical extreme of such a method would undoubtedly be the attempt to give up all resemblance to natural form, and to create a purely abstract language of form — a visual music; and the later works of Picasso show this clearly enough . . .

All art depends upon cutting off the practical responses to sensations of ordinary life, thereby setting free a pure and as it were disembodied functioning of the spirit . . .

Leonard Woolf, Beginning Again, An Autobiography of the Years 1911 to 1918, *1964*
. . . The first job which I took was a curious one. The second Post-Impressionist Exhibition, organized by Roger Fry, opened in the Grafton Galleries in the autumn of 1912. In Spain on our honeymoon I got an urgent message from Roger asking me whether I would act as secretary of the show on our return. I agreed to do so until, I think, the end of the year. It was a strange and for me new experience. The first room was filled with Cézanne water-colours. The highlights in the second room were two enormous pictures of more than life-size figures by Matisse and three or four Picassos. There was also a Bonnard and a good picture by Marchand. Large numbers of people came to the exhibition, and nine out of ten of them either roared with laughter at the pictures or were enraged by them. The British middle class — and, as far as that goes, the aristocracy and working class — are incorrigibly philistine, and their taste is impeccably bad. Anything new in the arts, particularly if it is good, infuriates them and they condemn it as either immoral or ridiculous

or both. As secretary I sat at my table in the large second room of the galleries prepared to deal with enquiries from possible purchasers or answer any questions about the pictures . . . Hardly any of them made the slightest attempt to look at, let alone understand, the pictures, and the same inane questions or remarks were repeated to me all day long. And every now and then some well groomed, red faced gentleman, oozing the undercut of the best beef and the most succulent of chops, carrying his top hat and grey suede gloves, would come up to my table and abuse the pictures and me with the greatest rudeness . . .

Roger Fry to Lady Fry   *Durbins, 9 November 1911*

. . . My work at the Borough Polytechnic has been a great success, at least in arousing interest. They had a great debate on it the other night which I was asked to open. It was a very amusing occasion with much freedom of speech, but on the whole they seemed inclined to be converted to my view. The Press has been almost entirely on my side. The Grafton Galleries are fairly successful — not quite so good as we had hoped, but we have already paid expenses so that the National Art-Collections Fund will probably get about £1000. I am lecturing at the Slade again; so you see, I'm fairly fully occupied . . .

Roger Fry to Vanessa Bell   *G.N.R. That means Great Northern Railway (1912?)*

. . . Oh Nessa, it was good, our little married life, and no one but you could have brought it off. I look at the drawings which malign you so but still do remind me of the sight of you on the black sofa. Nessa, I should be a real artist, really truly and without doubt if I could draw you often, because you have this miracle of rhythm in you, and not in your body only, but in everything you do. It all has the same delightful reasonableness, and, after all, beauty is a kind of reasonableness, you know. It means ease in all the things round you and in all your relations, so that even our relation, which isn't quite normal to either of us for we'd like the perfect ease and abandonment which we mustn't even think of ever having — even that becomes easy . . .

I like to think of you now, my dear, with your two cubs tucked into their beds and patted into shape like everything else in your desirable residence. And how you've dined alone and Sophie's given you a very long, very good, very solid and highly cooked dinner; and you've gone into the drawing room and patted everything once more to make it just right . . .

Leonard Woolf, Beginning Again, An Autobiography of the Years 1911 to 1918, *1964*

. . . One evening when he [Roger Fry] and Virginia and I were at Clive Bell's flat, a well-known politician, who was something of a buyer of pictures, came in after dinner accompanied by a large canvas. He wanted Roger's opinion as to whether the picture was or was not a Poussin. Roger examined it with the greatest care, but refused to commit himself. The picture was placed on the floor against the wall and we all began talking about something else. The conversation was general, but I noticed that, as it went on, all the time at intervals Roger's eyes wandered to the picture. After about an hour, Roger suddenly said that he had made up his mind, that it was not a Poussin. He then gave his reasons at great length;

he may or may not have been right, but the performance was extraordinarily convincing; it was an opinion based on expert knowledge and scientific investigation . . .

Roger Fry to G.L. Dickinson   *Durbins, 18 February 1913*

. . . I'm continuing my aesthetic theories and I have been attacking poetry to understand painting. I want to find out what the function of content is and am developing a theory which you will hate very much, *viz.*, that it is merely directive of form and that all the essential aesthetic quality has to do with pure form. It's horribly difficult to analyse, out of all the complex feelings just this one peculiar feeling; but I think that in proportion as poetry becomes more intense the content is entirely remade by the form and has no separate value at all. You see, the sense of poetry is analogous to the things represented in painting. I admit that there is also a queer kind of hybrid art of sense and illustration, but it can only arouse particular and definitely conditioned emotions, whereas the emotions of music and pure painting and poetry, when it approaches purity, are really free abstract and universal . . .

Roger Fry to Lady Fry   *Durbins, 28 March 1913*

Many many thanks for your kind and sympathetic letter. It is good of you to try to understand how things have affected me. I think it is likely, that in some ways, the great sorrow of Helen's loss and worse than loss has made me feel a great indifference to most of the things men work for. It has destroyed my own particular kind of home, tho' Joan [Fry, Roger's sister] does her very utmost to make up for it. Also it has made me feel no kind of ambition: any kind of success seems such a tiny thing compared with what I have lost; and with that a kind of recklessness perhaps which has enabled me to say what I really think about art without considering the consequences. All the same, I think if Helen had been well she would have encouraged me to take the line I have and would have faced the risk with me.

As to my being a failure, I am, from some points of view. I started to be an artist and I've never made a living by it. Then I got a big position as an authority on early art; but as you know, I didn't succeed in keeping my place in America and am out of the running for all official posts. I have been able to help others to get better positions than I could make for myself. No, I haven't got the kind of solid position which a man of my ability and age and experience may well expect. I meant failure from that point of view. As regards reputation, I'm not a failure. I suppose what I think has a great influence, though more with the rising generation than with my own. Certainly if influence is worth having, I've got that; and certainly I have accomplished a great deal for the understanding of art in England; but then I can quite see that, if one doesn't think that a very important thing, I haven't much to show for myself.

I think I have often seemed to you self-sufficient and headstrong when I have tried to explain my aims; but in fact, I am very conscious of my feebleness in many respects. After all, one has to make the best one can out of the materials of one's own nature.

But I do sincerely thank you, dear Mother, for showing me that you are willing to make allowances and to try to accept my work in life as having some meaning and value.

THE EARLY YEARS

DUNCAN GRANT
SELF-PORTRAIT, 1909

DUNCAN GRANT
STILL LIFE, 1907

DUNCAN GRANT
JOHN MAYNARD KEYNES, 1908

VANESSA BELL
PORTRAIT OF LYTTON STRACHEY, c.1912

VANESSA BELL
SAXON SYDNEY-TURNER. c.1910

VANESSA BELL
MRS ST JOHN HUTCHINSON, 1915

VANESSA BELL
PORTRAIT OF LYTTON STRACHEY READING, 1913

DUNCAN GRANT
THE KITCHEN, 1902

DUNCAN GRANT
CRIME AND PUNISHMENT, 1909

DUNCAN GRANT
LEMON GATHERERS, 1910

DUNCAN GRANT
PORTRAIT OF VIRGINIA WOOLF, 1911

ROGER FRY
CHAUVIGNY, 1911

ROGER FRY

WHITE ROAD WITH FARM, c.1912

ROGER FRY

BLACK SEA COAST, 1911

VANESSA BELL
VIRGINIA WOOLF AT ASHEHAM, c.1910

DUNCAN GRANT

THE TUB, 1912

DUNCAN GRANT
HEAD OF EVE. c.1912

DUNCAN GRANT
SOLOMON AND THE QUEEN OF SHEBA, 1912

DUNCAN GRANT

THE ASS, 1913

ROGER FRY
STILL LIFE: FLOWERS, c.1912

VANESSA BELL
SPANISH LADY. 1912

ROGER FRY
BOATS IN A HARBOUR, 1915

DUNCAN GRANT
VENUS AND ADONIS, c.1919

ROGER FRY
PAPER FLOWERS ON A MANTELPIECE. 1919

VANESSA BELL
HELEN DUDLEY, c.1915

ROGER FRY

SAMOTHRACE, 1913

ROGER FRY
SOUTH DOWNS. c.1917

VANESSA BELL
46 GORDON SQUARE. 1911

DUNCAN GRANT
THE MAT WORKER, 1915

DUNCAN GRANT
LYDIA LOPOKOVA, 1923

ROGER FRY
GOLDSWORTHY LOWES DICKINSON, 1925

ROGER FRY
SELF-PORTRAIT, 1918

DUNCAN GRANT
SELF-PORTRAIT, 1918

VANESSA BELL
ABSTRACT PAINTING, c.1914

DUNCAN GRANT
VANESSA BELL, 1915

VANESSA BELL
FREDERICK AND JESSIE ETCHELLS PAINTING, 1912

VANESSA BELL
STUDLAND BEACH, c.1912

VANESSA BELL
LANDSCAPE WITH HAYSTACK, c.1912

DUNCAN GRANT
ADRIAN STEPHEN. 1910

VANESSA BELL
STILL LIFE ON CORNER OF A MANTELPIECE, 1914

DUNCAN GRANT
THE MANTELPIECE, 1914

ROGER FRY
ROQUEBRUNE AND MONTE CARLO FROM PALM BEACH, 1915—16

VANESSA BELL
THE TUB, 1917

VANESSA BELL
STILL LIFE, MILK JUG AT ASHEHAM, 1917

ROGER FRY
STILL LIFE WITH T'ANG HORSE, c. 1919–21

DUNCAN GRANT
PORTRAIT OF IRIS TREE, 1913–15

EDWARD WOLFE
STILL LIFE WITH BOOKCOVER, 1918

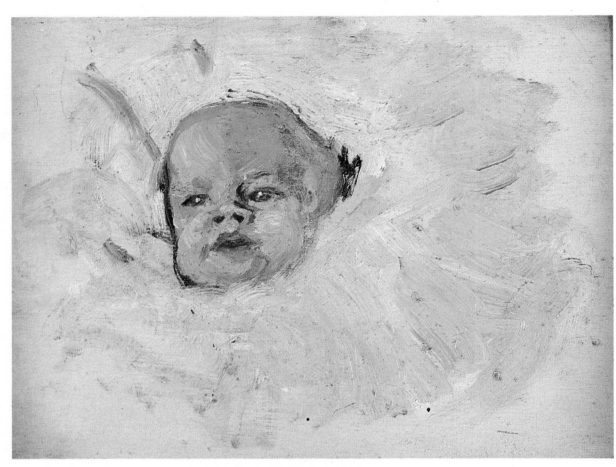

VANESSA BELL
JULIAN BELL, 1908

ROGER FRY
POPPIES AND IRISES, undated

DUNCAN GRANT
JULIAN BELL WRITING, 1928

DUNCAN GRANT
THE ARTIST'S MOTHER, 1918

VANESSA BELL AND DUNCAN GRANT

FOUR DOORS, c. 1921

THE OMEGA WORKSHOPS

THE OMEGA WORKSHOPS OPENED IN JULY 1913 IN FITZROY SQUARE (WITHIN WALKING DISTANCE OF BLOOMSBURY). THE IMPETUS FOR THEIR FORMATION AGAIN CAME FROM ROGER FRY, PARTLY IN RESPONSE TO PERSONAL (AND PUBLIC) REACTIONS TO THE POST-IMPRESSIONIST EXHIBITIONS, AND PARTLY AS A RESULT OF HIS CHAMPIONSHIP OF PENURIOUS YOUNG PAINTERS (INCLUDING VANESSA BELL AND DUNCAN GRANT) WHOSE WORK, HE BELIEVED, SHOWED 'STRONG DECORATIVE FEELING'.

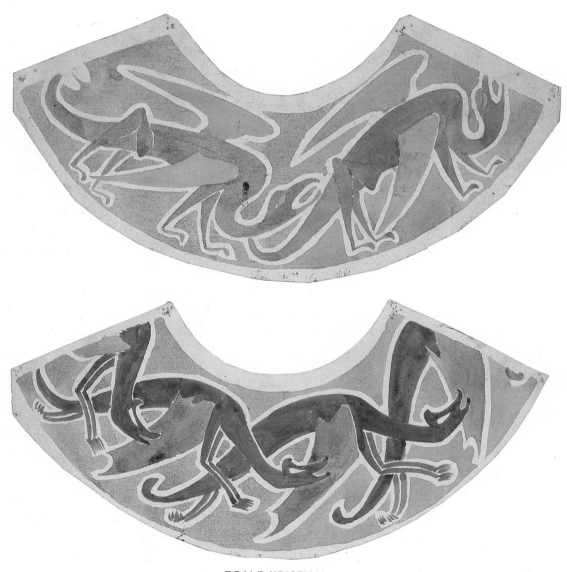

ROALD KRISTIAN

DESIGN FOR LAMPSHADE 'DRAGONS', 1915—16

Before launching the Workshops, Fry had had some experience of 'interior design'. He had built his own house, Durbins, furnishing it according to his ideals (see pages 60–61); as early as 1895 he had painted a mural in the house built by C.R. Ashbee for his mother on Cheyne Walk; and a year later Fry decorated the house of a friend, Hubert Crackanthorpe, 'with infinite care' (only to find that his client had destroyed all his 'schemes of colour' by hanging photographs around the rooms). Commissions such as these were similar to those carried out by Duncan Grant and Vanessa Bell for themselves and their friends; but the two projects which probably most influenced Roger Fry's ideals for the Workshops were the French *Ateliers Martine*, set up by the entrepreneurial couturier Paul Poiret in Paris in 1911, and the Borough Polytechnic commission which Fry had taken on in the same year. For the latter, which involved mural decorations in a students' dining room, Fry brought together several young painters, including Duncan Grant, Frederick Etchells, Bernard Adeney and Macdonald Gill (the brother of Eric Gill), who were to form the nucleus of the Omega team. Poiret's *Ateliers Martine*, on the other hand, was a more ambitious venture in which young working-class girls with no artistic training were employed: Poiret encouraged them to produce designs for fabrics and murals, as well as painted ceramics, rugs, carpets and furniture. Its success was due to the patronage of a sophisticated clientele more sympathetic than the British aristocracy to the experimental and the avant-garde.

Roger Fry, nevertheless, launched the Omega enterprise with his customary enthusiasm. His co-directors were Vanessa Bell and Duncan Grant, and other early participants included Wyndham Lewis and Eric Wadsworth. The 'Ideal Home Rumpus' which shattered this early collaboration was to have long-term implications (see the Introduction) but, as the following extracts indicate, the Workshops were to struggle on. Other collaborators included Nina Hamnett, Roald Kristian, Simon Bussy (who had married Dorothy Strachey, Lytton's sister), Henri Doucet, the young French painter, and the sculptor Henri Gaudier-Brzeska. Winifred Gill and Barbara Hiles (later Bagenal) were loyal helpers; Edward McKnight Kauffer and Paul Nash, who were later to establish reputations as artist-designers, were also involved.

The outbreak of war so soon after the Workshops were opened was disastrous on every level: Doucet and Gaudier-Brzeska were killed; Duncan Grant, as a conscientious objector, had to find work on a farm, and Vanessa went with him; and of course potential clients had less money to spend. The Workshops, nevertheless, produced textiles, ceramics, carpets and painted furniture, and also carried out some interesting commissions. Wealthy clients included Lady Ottoline Morrell, Lady Ian Hamilton, Lalla Vandevelde and Arthur Ruck. As well as the Ideal Home brief, Omega decorated a Cadena Café, and numerous exhibitions were held. By the end of 1919, however, it was obvious that the Workshops could not survive; a clearance sale had been held in July of that year, and the Omega Workshops went into voluntary liquidation a year later. Nonetheless the Omega idea did survive, not only at Charleston and in the 'degentrification' of interior design, but in the numerous campaigns throughout the twenties and thirties to involve artists in the design of everyday objects.

Artists and designers

Roger Fry, 'Art and Socialism', The Great State, 1912

. . . We are so far obliged to protect ourselves from the implications of modern life that without a special effort it is hard to conceive the enormous quantity of 'art' that is annually produced and consumed. For the special purpose of realizing it I take the pains to write the succeeding paragraphs in a railway refreshment-room, where I am actually looking at those terribly familiar but fortunately fleeting images which such places can afford. And one must remember that public places of this kind merely reflect the average citizen's soul, as expressed in his home.

The space my eye travels over is a small one, but I am appalled at the amount of 'art' that it harbours. The window towards which I look is filled in its lower part by stained glass; within a highly elaborate border, designed by someone who knew the conventions of thirteenth-century glass, is a pattern of yellow and purple vine leaves with bunches of grapes, and flitting about among these many small birds. In front is a lace curtain with patterns taken from at least four centuries and as many countries. On the walls, up to a height of four feet, is a covering of lincrusta walton stamped with a complicated pattern in two colours, with sham silver medallions. Above that a moulding but an inch wide, and yet creeping throughout its whole with a degenerate descendant of a Graeco-Roman carved guilloche pattern; this has evidently been cut out of the wood by machine or stamped out of some composition — its nature is so perfectly concealed that it is hard to say which. Above this is a wall-paper in which an effect of eighteenth-century satin brocade is imitated by shaded staining of the paper . . .

This painful catalogue makes up only a small part of the inventory of the 'art' of the restaurant. If I were to go on to tell of the legs of the tables, of the electric-light fittings, of the chairs into the wooden seats of which some tremendous mechanical force has deeply impressed a large distorted anthemion — if I were to tell of all these things, my reader and I might both begin to realize with painful acuteness something of the horrible toil involved in all this display. Display is indeed the end and explanation of it all. Not one of these things has been made because the maker enjoyed the making . . .

Roger Fry to G.B. Shaw   *11 November 1912*

. . . I am intending to start a workshop for decorative and applied art. I find that there are many young artists whose painting shows strong decorative feeling, who will be glad to use their talents on applied art both as a means of livelihood and as an advantage to their work as painters and sculptors.

The Post-Impressionist movement is quite as definitely decorative in its methods as was the Pre-Raphaelite, and its influence on general design is destined to be as marked. Already in France Poiret's Ecole Martine shows what delightful new possibilities are revealed in this direction, what added gaiety and charm their products give to an interior. My workshop would be carried on on similar lines and might probably work in conjunction with the Ecole Martine, by mutual exchange of ideas and products. I have also the promise of assistance from several young French artists who have had experience of such work: but in the main I wish to develop a definitely English tradition. Since the complete decadence of the Morris movement nothing has been done in England but pastiche and more or less unscrupulous imitation of old work. There is no reason whatever why people should not return to the more normal custom of employing contemporary artists to design their furniture and hangings, if only the artists can produce vital and original work.

The group of young artists who decorated the Borough Polytechnic [see page 123] a year ago have, I feel sure, the power to do this and have already formed the habit of working together with mutual assistance instead of each insisting on the singularity of his personal gifts. This spirit is of the utmost value in such decorative work as I propose, where co-operation is a first necessity. . . .

I calculate that the total expenses of running this workshop will be about £600 or £700 a year, I require about £2000 capital to give the scheme a fair chance: for at the end of three years it will be evident whether I am right in believing that there is a real demand for such work.

I propose to begin with those crafts in which painters can most easily and readily engage — the design of wall decorations in tempera and mosaic: of printed cotonnades: of silks painted in Gobelin dyes for curtains and dresses: painted screens: painted furniture. I hope to develop gradually the application of our designs to weaving, pottery and furniture construction . . .

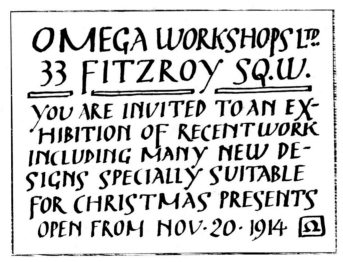

OMEGA INVITATION, 1914

Roger Fry to G.L. Dickinson   *Durbins, Sunday 31 May 1915*

. . . I've hardly known which way to turn since I've been back for the number of things to do and people to see. Most of all, I've had to work at the Omega Workshops, which is now fully started. It needs a tremendous lot of work to organize it properly. The artists are delightful people but ever so impractical. When I think of how practical the French artists are, I almost wish these weren't the delightful, vague, impossible Englishmen that they are . . . I've *got* to make it pay or goodness knows what'll become of me, let alone the group of artists who are already dependent on it. God knows how they lived before they got their thirty shillings a week from my workshop . . .

THE OMEGA WORKSHOPS SHOWROOM, 1913

Virginia Woolf, Roger Fry, A Biography, *1940*

. . . It [the Omega] showed signs of immediately becoming a great success. Orders were coming in. The public was amused and interested. The papers devoted a great deal of space to the new venture. Interviewers were sent to Fitzroy Square, and one of them has recorded his impressions of the Omega in those early days. Mr Fry, he says, took him round and he asked Mr Fry to explain his intentions. 'It is time', said Mr Fry, 'that the spirit of fun was introduced into furniture and fabrics. We have suffered too long from the dull and the stupidly serious.' He took up a wool work cushion. 'What do you think that represents?' said Mr Fry. 'A landscape?' the interviewer hazarded. Mr Fry laughed. 'It is a cat lying on a cabbage playing with a butterfly', he said . . . The interviewer looked and at last saw the butterfly though he failed to see the cat. Then Mr Fry showed him a chair. He said it was 'a conversational chair', a witty chair; he could imagine Mr Max Beerbohm sitting on it. Its legs were bright-blue and yellow, and brilliant bands of intense blue and green were worked round a black seat. Certainly it was much more amusing than an ordinary chair. Then there was a design for a wall decoration; a landscape with a purple sky, bright moon and blue mountains. 'If people get tired of one landscape', said Mr Fry, 'they can easily have another. It can be done in a very short time.' Then he brought out a screen upon which there was a picture of a circus. The interviewer was puzzled by the long waists, bulging necks and short legs of the figures. 'But how much wit there is in those figures', said Mr Fry. 'Art is significant deformity.' The interviewer was interested. Upstairs they went to the great white work-room, where one artist was at work upon a ceiling, another was painting what appeared to be 'a very large raccoon with very flexible joints' for the walls of a nursery. Then down again to the showroom where the journalist was made to look at chintzes, cushions, lamp-shades, garden tables and also 'a radiantly coloured dress of gossamery silk' designed by a French artist . . .

The 'Ideal Home Rumpus'

Frederick Etchells, C.J. Hamilton, Wyndham Lewis
and E. Wadsworth to possible patrons of
the Omega Workshops   1 Brecknock Studios, Brecknock Road, N. *[1912]*

        Understanding that you are interested in the Omega Workshops, we beg to lay before you the following discreditable facts.

    (1) That the Direction of the Omega Workshops secured the decoration of the 'Post Impressionist' room at the Ideal Home Exhibition by a shabby trick, and at the expense of one of their members — Mr Wyndham Lewis, and an outside artist — Mr Spencer Gore. The facts are as follows.

    Mr Spencer Gore was approached last July by the Agent of the *Daily Mail*, and . . . was invited, in conjunction with Mr Wyndham Lewis and Mr Roger Fry, to do a room for the Ideal Home Exhibition . . .

    Mr Gore was asked to arrange a meeting between the Agent of the *Daily Mail* and his colleagues. Immediately . . . he went on to the Omega Workshops, there seeing a director of the Company, and leaving word to the above effect; neither Mr Fry nor Mr Lewis being there at the time. Mr Lewis, then working at the Omega Workshops, would, he naturally thought, be at once communicated with. After that Mr Gore heard nothing further of the matter.

    Not only was this visit not mentioned to Mr Lewis, but the Direction at the Omega Workshops appropriated the commission, with the results at present visible to anyone visiting Olympia. As an example of the detailed working of this sordid game the following manoeuvre may be cited. When it was announced in the Workshop that the Ideal Home room had been secured by the 'Omega', and it came to apportioning the work, Mr Lewis was told by Mr Roger Fry that no decorations of any sort were to be placed on the walls, and was asked if he would carve a mantelpiece. Shortly after this, Mr Lewis went away on his holidays, and on his return in September, found large mural decorations, destined for the Olympia exhibition, around the walls of the workroom.

(2) A second unpleasant fact is the suppression of information in order to prevent a member from exhibiting in a Show of Pictures *not* organized by the Direction of the Omega. Mr Rutter, the Curator of the Leeds Art Gallery, in organizing a Post-Impressionist Exhibition in Bond Street, wrote to Mr Fry some weeks ago. In this letter he asked for Mr Etchell's address, wanting some of his work for the Exhibition. He was given to understand that Mr Etchells had no pictures ready and would have none till 1914. This statement of Mr Fry's was not only unauthorized but untrue. It is curious that a letter from Mr Rutter to Mr Lewis on the same subject, and addressed to the Omega Workshops, should never have reached him.

This mean and ludicrous policy of restraining artists might, perhaps, be justified if the Direction at all fulfilled its function of impresario: but its own Shows are badly organized, unfairly managed, closed to much good work for petty and personal reasons, and flooded with the work of well-intentioned friends of the Direction.

More incidents of the above nature could be alleged, but these two can be taken as diagnostics of the general tone of the place.

As to its tendencies in Art, they alone would be sufficient to make it very difficult for any vigorous art-instinct to long remain under that roof. The Idol is still Prettiness, with its mid-Victorian languish of the neck, and its skin is 'greenery-yallery', despite the Post-What-Not fashionableness of its draperies. This family party of strayed and Dissenting Aesthetes, however, were compelled to call in as much modern talent as they could find, to do the rough and masculine work without which they knew their efforts would not rise above the level of a pleasant tea-party, or command more attention.

The reiterated assurances of generosity of dealing and care for art, cleverly used to stimulate outside interest, have then, we think, been conspicuously absent in the interior working of the Omega Workshops. This enterprise seemed to promise, in the opportunities afforded it by support from the most intellectual quarters, emancipation from the middleman-shark. But a new form of fish in the troubled waters of Art has been revealed in the meantime, the Pecksniff-shark, a timid but voracious journalistic monster, unscrupulous, smooth-tongued and, owing chiefly to its weakness, mischievous.

No longer willing to form part of this unfortunate institution, we the undersigned have given up our work there.

Roger Fry to Spencer F. Gore   *The Omega, 5 October 1913*

Lewis tells me that you said you left a letter here from the Ideal Home Exhibition people asking Lewis to do decorations and asking the Omega to do the furniture. I told him that the *Daily Mail* people had approached me directly and that they had never mentioned his name. He thereupon doubted my word and said that I accused you of telling a lie; I wish to let you know in case he carries this to you that I repeatedly told him that I did not doubt your word but had no knowledge of any request that he should do the decorations as separate from the Omega. We should scarcely have thought of undertaking it,

OMEGA SITTING ROOM, IDEAL HOME EXHIBITION, 1913

if that had been the condition, as the Omega produces its work anonymously and would not expect to have the work distributed beforehand by outsiders among the various artists.

I have tried to treat Lewis with every consideration, but I fear nothing I can do comes up to his ideal of what is due to him. He has left, saying he will never come back, which I knew must happen sooner or later.

Roger Fry to Wyndham Lewis   *Omega Workshops Ltd. [1912]*

I find this afternoon, in packing up here to go away, the letter from Mr Rutter of which you spoke. I never saw it till now and can only suppose that you left it about and that it got put among my things. If this was due to my carelessness and want of method I am extremely sorry. I had read part of it before realizing it was addressed to you, and see that Mr Rutter has written to you before, so that I am glad to think that the accident of this letter getting mislaid here has not been, or need not have been, decisive in the matter of the exhibition.

Roger Fry to Duncan Grant   *Villeneuve les Avignon, October 1913*

Many thanks for your letter and all the bother and worry that you have gone through in fighting my battles. I think you've got to the bottom of the question. I suspect that Lewis has never been in the Omega except for what he could get out of it, and that even before we came back from Italy he had formed a 'cave'. I quite agree with you about Etchells; I always thought he would act on rather romantic impulses. The only thing is that I personally find it a little hard to think that he could turn so completely against me after having been so very friendly, and without ever listening to me. But I really want to help him and I quite expect that when he's seen the thing in a more reasonable way we shall be able to.

I've not heard a word about the Ideal Home. Has it been a success, and has there been any decent Press on it? . . .

. . . I have come definitely to the conclusion that the painting of pictures is too difficult a job for human beings. It's evident from the history of art that you can sink such an amount of talent and taste and thought and feeling in producing something completely tiresome; wherefore, I rejoice in the Omega because it is not beyond the wit of man to make a decent plate or a decent stuff . . .

DUNCAN GRANT
BEDHEAD DESIGN: RECUMBENT FEMALE, 1913

Roger Fry to Spencer F. Gore   *Villeneuve les Avignon, 18 October 1913*

Thanks for your letter. I appreciate your frankness in telling me that you uphold Lewis. I don't of course know why you believe him rather than me, but I can't help it if I am less persuasive. I can only repeat to you that everything I said is true, that Lewis did express himself to me as delighted to do the carving. If he really was not, I can only say that he was not frank with me. I shouldn't have had the slightest reason to make him do it; in fact,

I was perfectly willing to let him off at any time. I didn't tell him there would be no decoration. It is, I fear, useless for me to ask you to take my word for it, but I must in self defence tell you that this is so. The *Daily Mail* have fully confirmed my statement about the commission for the room . . .

Roger Fry to Lady Fry   *Durbins, 14 December 1913*

. . . I've a very hard time the last months; so hard that I'm giving up my lectureship at University College, which is more than I can manage, in order to see if I can pull through this venture of the Omega. It certainly arouses an immense amount of interest, but also a bitter opposition. I suppose it's natural that people should dislike it when you try to do something new, but I'm always a little surprised at the vehemence and the personal antagonism that it stirs up. Oddly enough, the people from whom I get most intelligent sympathy are our competitors in the trade. But I don't know why I run on about these things, except that one's mind is full of the effort just now. . . .

'SWIMMER' PENCIL BOX, 1913

'GOLDFISH' SEWING BOX, 1913

'It is fearfully exciting'

Roger Fry to Lady Fry   *Durbins, 14 June 1913*

. . . My Omega workshops are hard at work and keep me at it pretty continuously. There's a great deal of interest shown everywhere in the scheme and I hope I may be able to pull it through. If I do I shall I think have done something to make art possible in England. It would be of course almost to accomplish a miracle, but I have hopes. Certainly the people I have got have an extraordinary amount of talent. My problem is now to harness it to practical purposes. There's no doubt that it is a difficult thing to do and perhaps that is why almost all manufacturers give it up and go to the patient hack instead of the artist for their designs. . .

Winifred Gill to Duncan Grant   *April-August 1966*

. . . It is odd, but I have no recollection at all, at present, of the first time I saw 33 Fitzroy Square, but I remember clearly the all-out effort to get enough stuff ready for the opening.

. . . The walls of the back room were colour washed, distempered a warm puce. They were then decorated by Doucet . . . with sprays of leaves, each about eight feet long, stems and leaves were produced by templates . . . held against the wall and spattered all round with purple dye. I seem to remember a comb coming into the process somewhere. My part consisted in holding the step-ladder steady, not a very easy task because he was a small but vigorous and very active party . . .

WYNDHAM LEWIS
LAMPSHADE DESIGN, 1913

. . . We 'painted' cushion covers, scarves and lampshades in dyes on silk prepared by being brushed over by some paste or starch mixture brewed by Miles (the caretaker). At first this used to go bad very quickly, but later had something added to preserve it . . . The treatment rendered the silk as safe to paint on as paper, but [it] had to be sent to the Hampshire House Workshops at Hammersmith to undergo some treatment that fixed the dye and restored the texture. These workshops were run by Douglas Pepler . . .

... One morning soon after our opening, two ladies came into our showroom. I was rung for and came down to see what they wanted. They wished to see furniture. I showed them what we had. They were not satisfied. I had not shown them everything. I took them to the back showroom upstairs where there was some unfinished work. No — that was not what they had come for. Hadn't we some furniture that we didn't show everyone? There was as yet some unpainted furniture in the cellar. They inspected this. 'What's in here?' exclaimed one of them, suspiciously opening the door of a shallow shelved cupboard in the showroom. At last they rather shamefacedly said that they had heard that our furniture was 'immoral' and they wanted to see some. 'O', said I, 'that's only because we paint our chairs scarlet!' It was, I think, the *Morning Post* said that ...

... I don't remember ever being given any direction or the designs being criticized. The rather boring thing was that if a design became popular one had to keep copying it. We only copied our own designs with the single exception of a design of Vanessa's (for a lampshade) which had to be repeated in all sizes. It was a geometric design composed for straight lines only so that it lost nothing being copied...

... I see Jessie [Etchells], do you remember her, standing at the end of the kitchen table in the studio with her lovely pale gold hair parted smoothly on either side, her face, her milk white skin, pale pink cheeks and large pale blue eyes, and her beautiful slim figure. She was indolent in her movements and had a voice to match. I remember her saying once, 'I was thinking last night how dreadful it must be to grow old, and see desire fade from the eyes of men.' To which I naturally retorted, 'Wouldn't trouble me, I've never seen it there.' ...

... I remember G.B.S. [George Bernard Shaw] coming in one morning with his wife. He left all the talking to her. When they decided on your elephant tray, I remember that Roger Fry thought this was one of the best things we had done. 'Then kindly tell him that I picked it out myself without any prompting from you', he said. 'He always thinks I haven't any taste.' ...

... One afternoon I was taking a short rest ... in the back showroom ... suddenly the door burst open and in rushed Wyndham Lewis carrying a large paper bag which he threw on a small table. It is difficult now to credit that for a few weeks it was the fashionable thing to wear an outsize cloth cap, at least a foot across and made of a large black and white check material. Wyndham Lewis drew one of these out of the bag and tried it on in front of the long glass over the mantelpiece. He cocked it slightly to one side to his satisfaction, then, taking a few steps backward, raised his hand as though to shake hands with someone and approached the mirror with an ingratiating smile. He backed again and tried the effect of a sudden recognition with a look of surprised pleasure ...

... I seem to remember a long time painting the legs of tables. It had come as a surprise to me that black and white size paint would produce blue. When Venetian red was added, a warm mulberry colour resulted which I always connect with Vanessa. She was very fond of it, and we used it a good deal for background on our furniture. Trays too we painted, O yes, and endless candlesticks. When I remember Nina Hamnett at work it is always a candlestick she has in her hand ...

Wyndham Lewis, Rude Assignment, *1950*

        . . . with no preliminary workshop training it was idle to suppose that half a dozen artists could cope with all — or indeed any — of the problems of waxing, lacquering, polishing and varnishing of furniture . . . or the hand-painting of textiles which the plan involved. Naturally the chairs we sold stuck to the seats of people's trousers; when they took up an Omega candlestick they could not put it down again, they held it in an involuntary vice-like grip. It was glued to them and they to it.

Roger Fry to R.C. Trevelyan   *16 January 1914*

        . . . I've seen P. [Paul] Nash and arranged for him to come later on and try his hand at decorative work. We shall see how he turns out. It's a good test of where his real power lies. He has imagination of some kind if he can only find the way in which to use it. Also he's very sympathetic and I should like to have him with us. . . .

PAINTED LAMPSTANDS, 1913

Winifred Gill to Duncan Grant   *1966*

        . . . It was then [when the demand for pottery was expanding] that I thought of the Poole Potteries. The Carters were a family whom my brother had met. Roger wrote to Ronald Carter and received a friendly reply. Ronald Carter was invited to the Omega. The men shook hands and Roger said: 'The first thing I want to ask you, is what is your body like?' To which the reply was, rather surprisingly, 'Hard, quite hard, and I think I can promise you that it is water tight' . . .

Roger Fry to Duncan Grant   *1914*

   ... Vanessa and I have been potting all day and naturally talked much about you, so I was very glad to get your card when I got home.

   We went when the potter wasn't there and got the man to turn the wheel. It was fearfully exciting at first: the clay was too stiff and V. very nearly bust with the effort to control its wobbleliness — and in vain; then we got softer clay and both of us turned out some quite nice things — little ones only mostly, but they'll make quite nice little bowls and pots. It's fearfully exciting when you get it centred and the stuff begins to come up between your fingers. V. never would make her penises long enough which I thought very odd. Don't you? ...

   We saw Picasso's studio in Paris, but I expect Vanessa'll have told you about that ...

ROGER FRY
OMEGA SIX-SIDED VASE, 1913–19

Winifred Gill to Duncan Grant   *1966*

   ... By this time, August 1914, we sold a good many things beside our own stuff. Someone had advised Roger to go to a trade exhibition of textiles and he was delighted to find prints which Foxtons manufactured exclusively for the African market. The designs were strong and gay, and of necessity influenced by native taste ...

. . . Do you remember what trouble Roger had in getting our carpeting made up? The big English firms refused to touch them. One said he would not insult his workmen by asking them to carry out such ridiculous designs *. . .*

ROGER FRY
DESIGN FOR RUG FOR ARTHUR RUCK, 1916

Roger Fry to Vanessa Bell   *Bosham, 5 August 1916*
At the meeting of the Omega the accountant took a gloomy view of things. It appears that our expenses are about £360 a year on the lowest possible basis and this would require sales of £90 a month to cover. I doubt if we average £40. So the thing does seem rather hopeless as I don't think there can be any great revival after the war *. . .*

Roger Fry to Lady Fry   *Aldbourne, Wilts., 22 September 1916*
. . . I've really been quite hard worked with the Omega of late. I'm to have an exhibit of our things in the great arts and crafts exhibition at the RA. Isn't that amusing? But what was most amusing was the way in which the good people tried to leave me out and failed. I told them that it was a matter of complete indifference to me whether we showed or not, but that if we didn't show I should publicly contest any claim that their exhibition was representative of British applied art — whereupon they thought that the lesser evil was to give me a section to show in. I am now arranging it and hope to make some effect mainly by being so much soberer and more austere than my neighbours. *. . .*

Roger Fry to Vanessa Bell   *Durbins, 26 December 1918*

. . . As we can't get furniture made I've been buying old furniture and we are going to paint it up at the Omega. You might let people know if they want to get chairs, etc. . .

PAGE FROM *COLOUR MAGAZINE*, JUNE 1916

Roger Fry to Vanessa Bell   *21 Fitzroy Street, 11 March 1919*

. . .I'm nearly ruined by the Omega: find Paice has let the accounts go to pieces, the auditors furious, lots of old outstanding debts which I have to pay straight away, and most of our clients simply don't pay. I'm hideously overdrawn at the bank and owe heaps. It's terrible. But if I could only sell Durbins or let it, well, I could pull round. Only I must stop the Omega; but then I shall have to pay £500 at least to put the house right, which I simply don't know how to do . . . Then there are awful rows about the *Burlington* and a general atmosphere of hatred and fury against me among the cultured, who (Tonks & Co.) are nevertheless moving heaven and earth to get a Gauguin bought for the NG [National Gallery] apparently quite oblivious of the fact that I was turned out of polite society for having a show of him and that they raged with fury at them. Now they accept Gauguin but hate their contemporaries nonetheless . . .

PART IV

CHARLESTON

VANESSA BELL MOVED INTO CHARLESTON WITH DUNCAN GRANT, DAVID (BUNNY) GARNETT AND HER TWO SMALL SONS IN SEPTEMBER 1916. PRIOR TO THAT THEY HAD BEEN LIVING AT WISSETT LODGE IN SUFFOLK, WHERE DUNCAN GRANT AND DAVID GARNETT, AS CONSCIENTIOUS OBJECTORS, HAD BEEN EMPLOYED AS FARM-WORKERS. CHARLESTON, ALTHOUGH 'BY NO MEANS A GENTLEMAN'S HOUSE', OFFERED CERTAIN ADVANTAGES: FORMERLY USED AS A BOARDING HOUSE, IT WAS LARGE AND UNPRETENTIOUS, WITH THE POTENTIAL FOR STUDIOS AS WELL AS THE ABSORPTION OF LARGE NUMBERS OF PEOPLE; THE RENT WAS LOW; AND SINCE BOTH HOUSE AND GARDEN HAD BEEN NEGLECTED, THERE WAS AMPLE SCOPE FOR CREATIVE REGENERATION.

VANESSA BELL
PAINTED DOOR, DUNCAN GRANT'S BEDROOM, CHARLESTON 1916/18

CHARLESTON

Although the house was isolated (not necessarily a disadvantage), Virginia and Leonard Woolf had been living nearby since 1911. Roger Fry rented a farm in the vicinity, and Maynard Keynes, so frequent a guest that he had a room of his own there, took a lease on a house a few miles away when he married the ballet dancer Lydia Lopokova in 1925.

During the war years Vanessa and Duncan used what little spare time they had to continue painting; they also began to work on the house itself, and to buy what David Garnett described as 'hideous objects of furniture', transforming them into 'delightful works of art'. Clive Bell, who had already published *Art* in 1914, worked on his planned 'Great Book' *The New Renaissance* (to be reworked as *Civilization*) during his visits there. Probably the most influential book written at Charleston, however, was Maynard Keynes's *The Economic Consequences of the Peace*, written and published in 1919.

After the War, the household migrated between London and Charleston, with frequent visits abroad. Constant visitors during the summers spent at Charleston included original members of the Bloomsbury Group as well as new affiliations (see Clive Bell's essay on Bloomsbury). Dora Carrington came once with Lytton Strachey, and Roger Fry's new love, Helen Anrep, was a more frequent visitor after they began living together in 1926. Desmond and Molly MacCarthy, and Raymond Mortimer, were also regular guests, and Mary Hutchinson, Clive Bell's mistress, also braved the household's somewhat unconventional attitude to comfort, and then, of course, there were the children. Julian was eight when Vanessa moved to Charleston, and Quentin was six. Angelica, the daugher of Duncan Grant, was born there on Christmas Day 1918, and nearly died in her early months because of wrong medical advice. Her accounts of growing up in Charleston give a child's impression of its mystery and its enchantments, and of the working days there.

On the surface, therefore, this was an enviable life of creative activity, travel, children and friendship. But there was darkness as well, particularly for Vanessa who had to run this large household: she was concerned about Virginia's health, Duncan's absences and her children's futures, and they were all desolated by Roger Fry's sudden death in 1934, following a fall. Julian was especially close to his mother, but more politically committed than his Bloomsbury elders and impatient to break free. He went to Cambridge (where he became an Apostle), and in 1935 left for China to take up a post at the University of Wuhan. Two years later he was killed driving an ambulance in the Spanish Civil War. This meaningless extinction of a future, a repetition of the death of Thoby Stephen (and of countless others in the First World War) devastated Vanessa, and Charleston is full of reminders of this lost son.

Charleston survives, however, as a vibrant and appropriate memorial to the life there. Its decoration was a continuous process, with Quentin and Angelica also contributing. Roger Fry designed and helped to build the large studio; the paintings and decorations record friendships as well as the persistent activity. The house and the garden have now been restored by the Charleston Trust, who maintain the property and open it to the public.

Transforming Charleston

Virginia Woolf to Vanessa Bell   *Hogarth House, Richmond, 14 May [1916]*

    ... I wish you'd leave Wissett, and take Charleston. Leonard went over it, and says it's a most delightful house and strongly advises you to take it. It is about a mile from Firle, on that little path which leads under the downs. It has a charming garden, with a pond, and fruit trees, and vegetables, all now rather run wild, but you could make it lovely ...

Virginia Woolf to Vanessa Bell   *Carbis Bay, Cornwall, Sunday [24 September 1916]*

    It is very exciting to think that you may get Charleston. I hope you will. Leonard says there are certainly 8 bedrooms, probably more, and very good ones, two big sitting rooms on the ground floor and one small one; and very good large rooms on the first floor. He says the garden could be made lovely — there are fruit trees, and vegetables, and a most charming walk under trees. The only drawbacks seemed to be that there is cold water, and no hot, in the bathroom; not a very nice w.c. and a cesspool in the tennis court ... Whatever you may say, I think the country there is superb to live in — I always want to come back again, and one never feels it dull, but then, not being an artist, my feelings are not to be considered ha! ha! ... Please write soon and say what happens. I'm sure, if you get Charleston, you'll end by buying it forever. If you lived there, you could make it absolutely divine.

Vanessa Bell to Roger Fry   *October/November 1916*

    ... It really is so lovely that I must show it to you soon. It's absolutely perfect I think ... It has been refaced with some kind of quite harmless stucco plaster and has a creeper over it ... I suppose it's seventeenth or early eighteenth century (but my word doesn't go for much), anyhow it's most lovely, very solid and simple with flat walls in that lovely mixture of brick and flint that they use about here — and perfectly flat windows in the walls and wonderful tiled roofs. The pond is most beautiful with a willow at one side and a stone — or flint — wall edging it all round the garden part and a little lawn sloping down to it. Then there's a small orchard and the walled garden like the Asham one and another lawn or bit of field railed in beyond. There's a wall of trees — one single line of elms all round two sides which shelters us from west winds. We are just below Firle Beacon — which is the highest point on the downs near and except towards the downs the ground slopes down from the house on all sides. Inside the house the rooms are very large — and a great many. Ten bedrooms I think some enormous. One I shall make into a studio. It is very light and large with an east window but the sun doesn't come in much after quite early in the morning and it has a small room off it with another window. So we might get interesting interiors I think. The house is really much too large at present of course — but it's nice to have space and no doubt it will get filled in time. There's hardly any furniture in it yet. I am going into Lewes today to buy a few necessary things. The Omega dinner service looks most lovely in the dresser ...

David Garnett, The Flowers of the Forest, 1955

... The actual move which followed was not so easy. Charleston had to be furnished and made habitable: the children, servants, and ducks had to be moved from Wissett, to say nothing of the easels, scores of canvases, boxes of paints, packing cases of books and a sack of globe artichoke suckers ... At first there was an acute shortage of furniture and for some weeks Duncan and I had to sleep on the floor, owing to the lack of beds. For a long while several of the rooms remained empty and unused. Then some furniture was brought down from 46 Gordon Square, other pieces were bought in Lewes and these with rare exceptions were astounding objects, bargains which attracted Duncan or Vanessa because of their strange shapes and low prices ... Both Duncan and Vanessa appeared to believe that the inherent horror of any badly designed and constructed piece of furniture could be banished forever by decoration. The strange blend of hideous objects of furniture, painted with delightful works of art, gives to the rooms at Charleston a character which is unique and astonishing ...

VANESSA BELL
CUPBOARD, CHARLESTON, 1917

From Virginia Woolf's diary   *Friday 2 November* [1917]

    . . . Yesterday it rained all day, so I sat in; writing about Aksakoff in the morning; sitting in the Studio after luncheon. Duncan painted a table, and Nessa copied a Giotto *. . .* They are very large in effect, these painters; very little self-conscious; they have smooth broad spaces in their minds where I am all prickles and promontories. Nevertheless to my thinking few people have a more vigorous grasp or a more direct pounce than Nessa. Two little boys with very active minds keep her in exercise. I like the feeling that she gives of a whole nature in use. In working order I mean; living practically, not an amateur, as Duncan and Bunny [David Garnett] both to some extent are of course. I suppose this is the effect of children and of responsibility, but I always remember it in her *. . .*

VANESSA BELL

WINDOW OF THE SPARE ROOM, CHARLESTON, 1936

Roger Fry to Margery Fry   *Bo Peep Farm, Alciston, Sussex, 2 June 1918*

... I lead a very retired and quiet existence here — not quite hermitlike, for I'm near to Charleston, where Vanessa Bell and D. Grant live, and go in occasionally. Tho' I don't ever really see her so. The only way is to get her out of her domestic hole — she's too absorbed in that to really notice one's existence, so that I get very little out of it. I'm painting hard at landscape, done a few, I think some good, but I can't take the next step, which would be my inevitable synthesis and not a willed and deliberate one. Still I'm content to go on working at Nature almost literally, as tho' I'd several more lifetimes to do the trick in. If it ever comes with me it'll come horribly late — too late perhaps to come at all. It's queer that I do go on in spite of days of horrible doubt and depression ...

VANESSA BELL
DOOR IN THE SPARE ROOM, CHARLESTON, 1936

David Garnett, The Flowers of the Forest, *1955*

            Charleston was at first a rambling old farmhouse, full of badly planned passages and small rooms. There was, on the garden side, a long cool dairy room with solid slate slabs round the walls to set the shallow pans of milk for creaming; on the way to it was a pantry and another larder or a stillroom with a slatted door. Slowly the house took on another, but equally living character. One after another the rooms were decorated and altered almost out of recognition as the bodies of the saved are said to be glorified after the resurrection. Duncan painted many of the doors with pictures on the panels and with decorative borders round the frames. In every leisure moment he was at work . . . Duncan, like a sailor, was always quietly occupied with some task of his own invention. 'Creative activity was his passion; he was never satisfied with what he had ready-made; he longed to make something new.' Those words written of Tchehov were equally true of Duncan . . .

WINDOW IN CLIVE BELL'S STUDY, CHARLESTON

In his schemes Duncan was always seconded by Vanessa; they painted together in harmony, perfectly happy while they were at work, and rarely resting from it. Thus Charleston was transformed.

Then Clive took possession of one room with his shelves of books, boxes of cheroots, Rose Geranium bath salts and a guncase; the children filled others with toys; and, as they grew larger, fishing rods, butterfly nets, boats and an air-gun made their appearance . . .

Vanessa Bell to Roger Fry   [March 1918]

... Maynard came back suddenly and unexpectedly late at night having been dropped at the bottom of the lane by Austen Chamberlain in a Government motor and said he had left a Cézanne by the roadside! Duncan rushed off to get it and you can imagine how exciting it all was ...

CLIVE BELL'S STUDY. CHARLESTON

Children at Charleston

THE STUDIO, CHARLESTON

CHARLESTON

David Garnett to Constance Garnett   *Charleston, Christmas Day* [1918]

Dearest Mother, Vanessa had a daughter born at 2 a.m. this morning, so I am very glad I was here. It is a queer little creature, very lovely and full of independent life. I went for the doctor about nine and sat up till it was over and then was able to have a look at it. It weighed seven and a half pounds, being put in a cardboard box on the kitchen scales. Clive is very glad it is a girl; so will Virginia be for she thinks highly of her own sex. Vanessa doesn't and is probably rather disappointed.

It is a curious emotional experience waiting for someone else's child to be born.

Virginia Woolf to Violet Dickinson   *Hogarth House, 8 May 1919*

. . . I saw my new niece, Angelica, the other day; very lovely with vast blue eyes, and long fingers. Nessa presides over the most astonishing ménage; Belgian hares, governesses, children, gardeners, hens, ducks, and painting all the time, till every inch of the house is a different colour . . .

From Virginia Woolf's diary   *Wednesday 5 March* [1919]

. . . Charleston is by no means a gentleman's house. I bicycled round there in a flood of rain, & found the baby asleep in its cot, & Nessa & Duncan sitting over the fire, with bottles & bibs & basins all round them. Duncan went to make my bed. Their staff at this moment consists simply of Jenny, the sharp Jewish looking cook; & she having collapsed, spent the afternoon in bed. By extreme method & unselfishness & routine on Nessa's & Duncan's parts chiefly, the dinner is cooked, & innumerable refills of hotwater bottles & baths supplied. One has the feeling of living on the brink of a move. In one of the little islands of comparative order Duncan set up his canvas, & Bunny wrote a novel in a set of copy books. Nessa scarcely leaves the babies room, or if she appears for a moment outside, she has instantly to go off . . . to wash napkins, or bottles, or prepare meals . . .

Angelica Garnett, Deceived with Kindness, 1984

The studio was the citadel of the house, the sanctuary in which I spent the most treasured hours of my life. It was here, basking in the atmosphere of hard work and concentration, that I felt the most important things would happen; I was a dragonfly that hovers, disappears and returns, a law unto itself. As in a hothouse, I was both protected and stimulated, without a shadow of responsibility. I can imagine nothing better than sitting on the studio floor engrossed in some manual occupation while those patient elders concentrated in their own dreamlike fashion on their art. I absorbed so much in that atmosphere that I afterwards valued, aware that it was a privilege to have been there, but it was a little like giving a child strong alcohol — I was drunk with the attention bestowed on me and the expectation so strongly projected that I should behave like a grown-up, while at the same time everyone was ready to give in to my slightest whim. Two dovetailed attitudes were at work, the one born of a tolerance of childish behaviour, the other of a feeling that I should do better not to be a child at all . . .

Julian Bell, Essays, Poems and Letters, *1938*

AUTOBIOGRAPHY

I stay myself — the product made
By several hundred English years,
Of harried labourers underpaid,
Of Venns who plied the parson's trade,
Of regicides, of Clapham sects,
Of high Victorian intellects,
Leslie, FitzJames:

And, not among such honoured, marbled names,
That cavalry ruffian, Hodson of Hodson's Horse,
Who helped take Delhi, murdered the Moguls;
At least a soldiering brigand: there were worse,
Who built a country house from iron and coal:
Hard-bitten capitalists, if on the whole
They kept the general average of their class.

And then, not breeding but environment,
Leisure without great wealth; people intent
To follow mind, feeling and sense
Where they might lead, and, for the world, content
To let it run along its toppling course.
Humane, just, sensible; with no pretence
To fame, success, or meddling with that world.

And one, my best, with such a calm of mind,
And, I have thought, with clear experience
Of what is felt of waste, confusion, pain,
Faced with a strong good sense, stubborn and plain;
Patient and sensitive, cynic and kind.

The sensuous mind within preoccupied
By lucid vision of form and colour and space,
The careful hand and eye, and where resides
An intellectual landscape's living face,
Oh certitude of mind and sense, and where
Native I love, and feel accustomed air.

And then the passage of those country years,
A war-time boyhood; orchard trees run wild,
West wind and rain, winters of holding mud,
Wood fires in blue-bright frost and tingling blood,
All brought to the sharp senses of a child . . .

Peace for the painters?

DUNCAN GRANT
THE GARDEN ROOM FIREPLACE, CHARLESTON

Clive Bell to Vanessa Bell   [? December] 1916

   . . . There was only one thing I didn't like at Charleston: need you do
so much house-work? Because the bloody government has made slaves of Duncan and
Bunny, need it make one of you? And why don't you paint more?

PART IV

WINDOW IN DUNCAN GRANT'S BEDROOM, CHARLESTON

Roger Fry to Vanessa Bell   *Durbins, 16 September 1917*

. . . Oh, why do I admire you? My dear, it would take ages to tell you all I do admire you for; but you see, I think you go straight for the things that are worth-while — you have done such an extraordinarily difficult thing without any fuss: cut thro' all the conventions, kept friends with a pernickety creature like Clive, got quit of me and yet kept me your devoted friend, got all the things you need for your own development and yet managed to be a splendid mother — no, you really can't wonder. You give one a sense of security, of something solid and real in a shifting world. I know that for me that's been to some extent an illusion: it was the curious feeling that I'd found what was absolutely necessary to me in you and that that was permanent and solid that made the break up so terrific when it came. You had made me feel so strangely secure, but now again I feel it, though I know it can't seriously

affect my life. Then to your marvellous practical power, which has, of course, really a quality of great imagination in it, because your efficiency comes without effort or worry or fuss. No, I don't think you need ever doubt yourself. You have genius in your life as well as in your art and both are rare things, so you can feel pretty well pleased with yourself. I who have no trace of genius anyhow, can't help a deep envy of your gifts . . .

Roger Fry to Vanessa Bell   *Morbihan, 3 or 4 September 1920*

. . . I wish you wouldn't always paint your best things just to decorate odd corners of your house . . .

DUNCAN GRANT
DOG MURAL, THE LIBRARY, CHARLESTON, c.1916—17

From Virginia Woolf's diary   *Monday 6 August* [1923]

We went over to Charleston yesterday. Although thinking quite well of ourselves, we were not well received by the painters. There they sat like assid[u]ous children at a task in a bedroom — Roger, Nessa, & Duncan; Roger on chair in foreground; Nessa on sofa, Duncan on bed. In front of them was one jar of flowers, & one arrangement of still life. Roger was picking out his blue flower very brightly. For some reason, the talk was not entirely congenial. I suspect myself of pertness and so on. Clive was sitting in the drawing room window reading Dryden . . .

Friday 25 August [1924]

. . . Charleston is as usual. One hears Clive shouting in the garden before one arrives. Nessa emerges from a great variegated quilt of asters and artichokes; not very cordial; a little absent minded. Clive bursts out of his shirt; sits square in his chair and bubbles. Then Duncan drifts in, also vague, absent minded, and incredibly wrapped round with yellow waistcoats, spotted ties, and old blue stained painting jackets. His trousers have to be hitched up constantly. He rumples his hair. However, I can't help thinking that we grow in cordiality, instead of drifting out of sight. And why not stand on one's own legs, and defy them, even in the matter of hats and chaircovers? Surely at the age of forty . . .

DUNCAN GRANT
PAINTED DOOR, CLIVE BELL'S STUDY, CHARLESTON

As for Duncan he requires, I think, peace for painting. He would like it all settled one way or the other. We saw a perfectly black rabbit, and a perfectly black cat, sitting on the road, with its tail laid out like a strap.

'What they call an example of melanism' said Clive — which amused me very much, and also made me like him . . .

CHARLESTON

Roger Fry to Helen Anrep *Charleston, 18 April 1925*

. . . Here we sit and shiver except when Vanessa and I are forced to go out in the back yard and try to measure the area of her projected studio with a broken tape measure, which is all that the place affords. However bit by bit we are conceiving a grand scheme and I've at last finished the plans, elevation and details. It's really the humblest architectural effort you can imagine, for the great object is to have as much room and spend as little money as possible. That, of course, appeals to my avaricious nature, which is almost as gratified by saving other people's money as my own. Anyhow it's great fun trying to make use of all the queer shapes of wall that these sheds and outhouses provide and drawing them together into a single building. We're also going to use the old tiles — so that what with old tiles and old flint walls, even though there's no architectural 'features', it may make a quite decent sort of barn and if we can keep the builder from putting in knick-knacks and mouldings, why it may be respectable and, God knows, it ought to be cheap . . .

DUNCAN GRANT
'ACROBAT' DOOR PANEL, CLIVE BELL'S STUDY, CHARLESTON, 1958

A paradise of the senses

Clive Bell, Old Friends, *1956*

. . . At Charleston it was our habit to sit after dinner in an oblate semi-circle before a curious fire-place, devised and constructed by Roger Fry to heat with logs a particularly chilly room: strange to say, it did. Each of us would be reading his or her book, and someone was sure to be reading French . . .

. . . For my part I never cared about playing chess with Roger; if, by any chance, one succeeded in some little plot for surprising his queen or rook — and setting traps is what amuses all thoroughly bad players such as I — he would dismiss the strategem as 'uninteresting', retract a series of moves — generally to his own advantage — and so continue till on scientific and avowable principles he had beaten one to his satisfaction. . .

VANESSA BELL AT CHARLESTON, 1930

Angelica Garnett, Deceived with Kindness, *1984*

. . . There was however one man about whom I had no reservations, and that was Roger Fry. Equally welcome to both painters and writers, his arrival at Charleston was always an occasion for joy and sometimes amusement . . .

To me he was a grandfather with paternal and avuncular overtones, whom I had no qualms in asking to perform miracles. Thus he would teach me to tie knots designed never to come undone, make for me paper birds that flew, stick things together for me without the faintest sign of impatience, his deep voice purring gently, a forgotten smile hovering over his features. His attitude to making things was very different from that of Vanessa and Duncan. Duncan was like a child: his nails and glue were made of faith, and if this failed he simply laughed. Vanessa was more practical — indeed the curtain rods she hung from twisted nails and bits of

string are still in place at Charleston — but Roger had theories and had to prove them, so that everything he made for me had the double fascination of being a game for me and an experiment intended for his own satisfaction . . .

. . . Life at Charleston continued, bathed it seemed in the glow of a perpetual summer. The household fell into two halves: on the one hand the painters, on the other the writers. If we lived happily together it was largely because, like birds or animals, we each had our own territory, duly respected by the others. Within a domestic framework, rhythmic and reassuring, we all had space and liberty to pursue our own interests, meeting at regular intervals in the dining-room to be sociable and convivial.

Vanessa presided in the dining-room, the magnetic centre of all our thoughts and activities. At breakfast she was always down first and sat for some time alone, enjoying her solitude. She had dressed and washed quietly, almost secretively, and would be in her habitual place on the far side of the round table, looking with dreamy reflectiveness at the still-life in the centre, or out of the window at the pond and the weather. Her gestures, for the most part slow and even cumbrous, would suddenly reveal her as a girl — virginal and inexperienced. Age showed itself, however, in her furrowed forehead, in the tortoiseshell spectacles balanced on the curve of her nose, and the deep vertical lines between her eyes which recalled that life was uphill, sometimes painful. Nevertheless she was enjoying herself. The luxuries she would have asked for on her desert island would have been a picture by Giotto, and unlimited quantities of black coffee . . .

On Vanessa's emergence from the kitchen she and Duncan would retire down the long passage to the studio, which was half work-room and half sitting-room, redolent of oil and turpentine. Easels and paintboxes stood about, brushes, sometimes festooned with cobwebs, emerged from jugs or jam jars, palettes and tubs of paint lay on stools or tables, while there was often a bunch of red-hot pokers and dahlias arranged in front of a piece of drapery. The gun-powder-coloured walls were hung with canvases of many shapes and sizes, and some of Duncan's favourite objects, such as a jointed — or rather disjointed — Sicilian wooden horse, a silver table-watch once given by her admirers to Lydia Lopokova [wife of Maynard Keynes], a fan and perhaps a child's drawing, could be seen balanced on the mantelpiece or pinned to a spare piece of wall.

On either side of the large stove were two chairs where they sat, Vanessa smoking the first of her self-imposed allowance of cigarettes, Duncan one of an endless chain always hanging from his lips . . .

John Lehmann, The Whispering Gallery, *1955*

. . . The half-finished canvases by Duncan Grant, or Julian's mother Vanessa, or his brother Quentin piled carelessly in the studios, and the doors and fireplaces of the old farm-house transformed by decorations of fruit and flowers and opulent nudes by the same hands, the low square-tables made of tiles fired in Roger Fry's Omega workshops, and the harmony created all through the house by the free, brightly coloured post-impressionist style that one encountered in everything from the huge breakfast cup one drank one's coffee from to the bedroom curtains that were drawn in the morning, not by a silent-footed valet or housemaid but by one's own hand to let in the Sussex sunshine, excited the suppressed painter that lurked in my breast. They seemed to suggest how easily life could be restored to a paradise of the senses if one simply ignored the conventions that still gripped one in the most absurd ways, clinging from a past that had been superseded in the minds of people of clear intelligence and unspoilt imagination . . .

Paradise lost

Julian Bell, Notes for a Memoir, *from* Essays, Poems, Letters, *1938*

     . . . Looking back at it, my life seems to me to have been very unusually happy, and even successful: not that I have cut much figure in the world, but in that I have had what I really wanted — except war, which I hope to see before long. I fancy also that the impression I have made on others is of the kind I desire . . .

From Julian Bell to Vanessa Bell   *26 September 1935*
   Dearest Nessa

     I can't tell you how ridiculous I feel writing this at 9 o'clock in the morning and cold blood. But as I don't mean you ever to see it, or anyone: as I believe the probabilities are all that I shall be burning it in two or three years' time, I can get rid of my feeling of selfconsciousness.

     I don't know that China is likely to be so much more dangerous than England: I certainly don't mean to make it so. But it is a long way off, and if I do have any accident I should like to feel that I was able to communicate with you in this way . . .

     Well, when it comes to the point, what have I to say to you? Principally, I think, that I've had an extremely happy life, and done most of the things I've wanted to do. Of course, there's masses more I want, and I don't feel in the least tired or at an end. But looking back on it all, it seems to me fairly complete: I can't see anything very serious that I've missed, except perhaps marrying and having children, and that I've never yet wanted. Also, it's true, I am and always have been fundamentally ambitious; I should have liked more of the more obvious successes, and power. But I don't think I mind very much the thought of missing them . . .

     The other thing, which doesn't really need to be said between us, is that I love you more than anyone else, and always have done so, ever since I can remember. Also, that if I've managed to have a happy life I owe it more to you than anyone else — after you, perhaps to Roger and Bloomsbury and Cambridge. What I mean is that I seem to have learned from you my attitudes to life and the sort of things to value and ways to behave. . .

Angelica Garnett, Deceived with Kindness, *1984*

     . . . Appropriately enough, I was dancing at the London Theatre Studio in a dramatic ballet on the theme of Goya's *'Desastros della Guerra'*. It was my most

successful part and one I very much enjoyed. In June that year [1937] we gave a fortnight's showing to friends and public. One evening after the performance had started Duncan suddenly appeared in the narrow alleyway outside the theatre: Julian had been killed, would I come home immediately? . . .

I found Vanessa in bed, white and swollen with tears, almost unable to speak. I said I had known all the time that it would happen, and so did she, but apart from that first embrace we became no nearer to each other. Everyone's effort was strained towards her, longing but unable to comfort her. Only Virginia and Duncan were of some use to her. Although not a mother herself, Virginia was imaginative enough to understand the kind of agony Vanessa was going through and was unafraid to talk of the past. Duncan, as usual, preserved his

CLIVE BELL'S BEDROOM, CHARLESTON

extraordinary serenity. Clive, however, pretended to a distressing detachment at a moment when detachment was impossible.

Before long we were at Charleston again, and Vanessa lay on a daybed in the studio looking down the empty garden path, occasionally weeping, more often exhausted . . . In spite of Julian's recommendation, in a letter she was to receive after his death, that she should work, it was some time before she stood at her easel again. Slowly, however, she reoccupied her place in the household, fulfilling her previous duties in an effort to restore a normality to which we had all grown so accustomed that we could hardly recognize life without it. The effort she made must have helped her, but nothing could restore her previous confidence in life which had been born of a feeling that, doing no harm, we should not suffer much . . .

PEDESTAL BOOKCASE IN THE SPARE ROOM, CHARLESTON, 1920s

CHARLESTON

Virginia Woolf, A Memoir of Julian Bell, *30 July 1937*

I am going to set down very quickly what I remember about Julian, — partly because I am too dazed to write what I was writing: then I am so composed that nothing is real unless I write it. And again, I know by this time what an odd effect Time has: it does not destroy people — for instance, I still think perhaps more truly than I did, of Roger, of Thoby: but it brushes away the actual personal presence.

The last time I saw Julian was at Clive's, two days before he went to Spain. It was a Sunday night, the beginning of June — a hot night. He was in his shirtsleeves. Lottie was out, & we cooked dinner. He had a peculiar way of standing: his gestures were, as they say, characteristic. He made sharp quick movements, very sudden, considering how large & big he was, and oddly graceful. They reminded one of a sharp winged bird — one of the snipe here in the marsh. I remember his intent expression; seriously looking, I suppose at toast or eggs, through his spectacles. He had a very serious look . . . he held his own with Clive & L.: and was cool & independent. I felt he had met many different kinds of people in China. Anyhow, as it was hot, & they talked politics, V[anessa]. and A[ngelica]. & I went out into the Square, & then the others came, & we sat & talked. I remember saying something about Roger's papers, & telling Julian I should leave them to him in my will. He said in his quick way, Better leave them to the British Museum. & I thought, That's because he thinks he may be killed. Of course we all knew that this was our last meeting — all together — before he went . . .

I had determined not to think about the risks, because, subconsciously I was sure he would be killed; that is I had a couchant unexpressed certainty, from Thoby's death I think; a legacy of pessimism, which I have decided never to analyse. Then, as we walked towards the gate together, I went with Julian, and said, Won't you have time to write something in Spain? Won't you send it us? . . . And he said very quickly — he spoke quickly with a suddenness like his movements — 'Yes, I'll write something about Spain. And send it you if you like.' Do I said, & touched his hand. Then we went up to Clive's room: & then they went: we stood at the door to watch them. Julian was driving Nessa's car. At first it wouldn't start. He sat there at the wheel frowning, looking very magnificent, in his shirt sleeves; with an expression as if he had made up his mind & were determined, though there was this obstacle — the car wouldn't start. Then suddenly it jerked off — & he had his head thrown slightly back, as he drove up the Square with Nessa beside him. Of course I noted it, as it might be our last meeting. What he said was 'Goodbye until this time next year' . . .

From Virginia Woolf's diary   *Tuesday 12 October* [1937]

. . . With Thoby . . . I felt we were the same age. With Julian it is the old woman, saying that she won't see the young again. It is an unnatural death, his. I can't make it fit in anywhere. Perhaps because he was killed, violently. I can do nothing with the experience yet. It seems still emptiness: the sight of Nessa bleeding: how we watch: nothing to be done . . . But the future without Julian is cut off, lopped: deformed . . .

Tuesday 28 February [1939]

Yesterday, Franco was recognized. And Julian killed for this. Nessa though I suppose making herself live: succeeding: very busy.

THE HOGARTH PRESS

THE HOGARTH PRESS WAS ESTABLISHED AS AN AMATEUR VENTURE, ALMOST AS A THERAPEUTIC HOBBY, FOR VIRGINIA WOOLF. FROM THE OUTSET, HOWEVER, VIRGINIA AND LEONARD WOOLF WERE INNOVATORS IN THEIR CHOICE OF PUBLICATIONS, AS WELL AS IN PRESENTATION.

ROGER FRY
BOOKJACKET OF *LIVING PAINTERS*, 1923

In the first three years of the Press's existence they personally printed, bound and distributed work by T.S. Eliot, E.M. Forster and Katherine Mansfield, as well as by Virginia. It was no doubt their support and championship of young and at that time 'uncommercial' authors that ensured the Press's success: unlike the many 'private' presses established in the wake of the Arts and Crafts Movement, Hogarth was concerned with content rather than form, books, which, as Leonard put it, were intended to be read rather than looked at. As well as championing new writers like Eliot and Herbert Read (and later Stephen Spender, Christopher

Isherwood and C. Day Lewis), the Press published the *Collected Papers* of Sigmund Freud (in 1924); their lists, in fact, read like a roll-call of the thirties' avant-garde in literature (although, perhaps significantly, they had no time for James Joyce).

Leonard and Virginia first ran the Press from their home in Richmond, but by 1924 it had 'crept all over the house', and premises were leased at 52 Tavistock Square: Hogarth had migrated to Bloomsbury. Among the 'succession of young men' who worked there were 'Dadie' Rylands, who was to become a Cambridge don, the translator Angus Davidson, and Richard Kennedy, whose *A Boy at the Hogarth Press* is a delightful and irreverent account of life below stairs at Tavistock Square. The poet and writer John Lehmann also worked there in the late twenties and early thirties, becoming a partner in 1932.

The wartime and subsequent history of the Press is recounted by Leonard Woolf in the following brief extracts from his memoirs. In 1946 it became one of the subsidiary companies of Chatto & Windus and still survives under its own imprint today. A remarkable achievement for an enterprise which originated, to quote Leonard Woolf, as 'a personal fluke'.

The first four years

From Virginia Woolf's diary   *Monday 25 January 1915*

      . . . I don't know when I have enjoyed a birthday so much — not since I was a child anyhow. Sitting at tea we decided three things: in the first place to take Hogarth [House, in Richmond], if we can get it; in the second, to buy a Printing press; in the third to buy a Bull dog, probably called John. I am very much excited at the idea of all three — particularly the press. I was also given a packet of sweets to bring home. . .

Leonard Woolf, Beginning Again, An Autobiography of the Years 1911 to 1918, 1964

      . . . We were both interested in printing and had from time to time in a casual way talked about the possibility of learning to print. It struck me that it would be a good thing if Virginia had a manual occupation of this kind, which, in say the afternoons, would take her mind completely off her work. Towards the end of 1916 we definitely decided that we would learn the art of printing. But that proved to be not at all an easy thing to do . . . When we went to the St Bride's school of printing down Bride Lane, Fleet Street, we learned that the social engine and machinery made it impossible to teach the art of printing to two middle-aged middle-class persons. Printing could only be taught to trade union apprentices, the number of whom was strictly limited.

This seemed to end our career as printers before it could begin. But on March 23, 1917, we were walking one afternoon up Farringdon Street from Fleet Street to Holborn Viaduct when we passed the Excelsior Printing Supply Co. It was not a very large firm, but it sold every kind of printing machine and material, from a handpress and type to a composing stick. Nearly all the implements of printing are materially attractive and we stared through the window at them like two hungry children gazing at buns and cakes in a baker shop window . . . We went in and explained our desire and dilemma to a very sympathetic man in a brown overall. He was extremely encouraging. He could not only sell us a printing machine, type, chases, cases, and all the necessary implements, but also a 16-page pamphlet which would infallibly teach us how to print. There was no need to go to a school of printing or to become an apprentice; if we read his pamphlet and followed the instructions, we should soon find that we were competent printers. Before we left the shop we had bought a small hand-press, some Old Face type, and all the necessary implements and materials for a sum of £19. 5s. 5d. . . .

When the stuff was delivered to us in Richmond, we set it all up in the dining-room and started to teach ourselves to print. The Excelsior man proved to be right; by following the directions in the pamphlet we found that we could pretty soon set the type, lock it up in the chase, ink the rollers, and machine a fairly legible printed page. After a month we thought we had become sufficiently proficient to print a page of a book or pamphlet. We decided to print a paper-covered pamphlet containing a story by each of us and to try to sell it by subscription to a limited number of people whom we would circularize. Our idea, was that, if this succeeded, we might go on to print and publish in the same way poems or other short works which the commercial publisher would not look at.

We set to work and printed a 32-page pamphlet, demy octavo, with the following title page:

Publication No. 1

TWO STORIES

<small>WRITTEN AND PRINTED</small>

<small>BY</small>

VIRGINIA WOOLF

<small>AND</small>

L. S. WOOLF

HOGARTH PRESS

RICHMOND

· 1917

. . . We began to print *Two Stories* on May 3 in an edition of about 150 copies. We bound it ourselves by stitching it into paper covers. We took a good deal of trouble to find some rather unusual, gay Japanese paper for the covers. For many years we gave much time and care to finding beautiful, uncommon, and sometimes cheerful paper for binding our books, and, as the first publishers to do this, I think we started a fashion which many of the regular, old

established publishers followed. We got papers from all over the place, including some brilliantly patterned from Czechoslovakia, and we also had some marbled covers made for us by Roger Fry's daughter in Paris. I bought a small quantity of Caslon Old Face Titling type and used it for printing the covers . . .

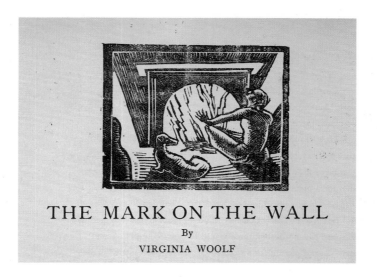

From Virginia Woolf's diary   *Tuesday 9 July* [1918]

           I can't fill up the lost days, though it is safe to attribute much space in them to printing. The title page was finally done on Sunday. Now I'm in the fury of folding & stapling, so as to have all ready for glueing & sending out tomorrow & Thursday. By rights these processes should be dull; but it's always possible to devise some little skill or economy, & the pleasure of profiting by them keeps one content. . .

DORA CARRINGTON

ILLUSTRATIONS FROM *TWO STORIES*, 1917

Leonard Woolf, Downhill All The Way. An Autobiography of the Years 1919 to 1939, *1967*

. . . In May 1919 we published in the Hogarth Press *Kew Gardens.* As I recorded in *Beginning Again,* this thin little volume, which we had printed ourselves, had great importance for us, for its immediate success was the first of many unforeseen happenings which led us, unintentionally and often reluctantly, to turn the Hogarth Press into a commercial publishing business. But it was also a decisive step in Virginia's development as a writer. It is in its own small way and within its own limits perfect; in its rhythms, movement, imagery, method, it could have been written by no one but Virginia . . .

Leonard Woolf, Beginning Again. An Autobiography of the Years 1911 to 1918, *1964*

. . . The expansion of the Press into something which we had never intended or originally envisaged can be seen in the following list of books published by us in the first four years of its existence:

1917.   L. and V. Woolf. *Two Stories.* Printed and bound by us.
1918.   K. Mansfield. *Prelude.* Printed and bound by us.
1919.   V. Woolf. *Kew Gardens.* 1st ed. printed and bound by us.
      T. S. Eliot. *Poems.* Printed and bound by us.
      J. Middleton Murry. *Critic in Judgment.* Printed for us.
1920.   E. M. Forster. *Story of the Siren.* Printed and bound by us.
      Hope Mirrlees. *Paris.* Printed and bound by us.
      L. Pearsall Smith. *Stories from the Old Testament.* Printed for us.
      Gorky. *Reminiscences of Tolstoi.* Printed for us.

From Virginia Woolf's diary   *Monday 2 August* [1920]

. . . As a hobby, The Hogarth Press is clearly too lively & lusty to be carried on in this private way any longer. Moreover, the business part of it can't be shared, owing to my incompetence. The future, therefore, needs consideration . . .

A mongrel in the business world

Leonard Woolf, Downhill All The Way. An Autobiography of the Years 1919 to 1939, *1967*

. . . The development of the Hogarth Press was bound up with the development of Virginia as a writer and with her literary or creative psychology. When we moved from Hogarth House, Richmond, to 52 Tavistock Square on March 13, 1924, the Hogarth Press had published 32 books in the seven years of its existence . . .

. . . The Hogarth Press, in these early years, met with a rather chilly welcome, or rather cold shoulder, from the booksellers. If you compare the thirteen books which we published in that

year [1923] with any thirteen similar books from other publishers, you will find that all of ours have something more or less unorthodox in their appearance. They are either not the orthodox size or not the orthodox shape, or their binding is not orthodox; and even worse, what was inside the book, what the author said, was in many cases unfamiliar and therefore ridiculous and reprehensible, for it must be remembered that, if you published 42 years ago poetry by T. S. Eliot, Robert Graves, and Herbert Read and a novel by Virginia Woolf, you were publishing four books which the vast majority of people, including booksellers and the literary 'establishment', condemned as unintelligible and absurd. . . . In 1923 we had no travellers and in a very desultory way we took our books round to the more important booksellers ourselves in order to get subscription orders before publication. It was a depressing business . . .

The Press was therefore a mongrel in the business world. We ran it in our spare time on lines invented by myself without staff and without premises; we printed in the larder, bound books in the dining-room, interviewed printers, binders, and authors in a sitting-room. I kept the accounts, records of sales etc., myself in my own way . . .

Lytton [Strachey] was eager that we should take Ralph [Partridge] into the Hogarth Press, first as an employee on trial, and with the prospect of ultimately becoming a partner. Eventually we agreed, and on August 31, 1920, the Press acquired its first paid employee . . .

From Virginia Woolf's diary   *Wednesday 16 August 1922*

    . . . A man called Whittall, wants to come in: young, intelligent, with a motor car, well dressed, sociable & critical; living in London & not pressed for money. I am a little alarmed by the social values of Mr W. for we don't want the Press to be a fashionable hobby patronized & inspired by Chelsea . . .

Leonard Woolf, Downhill All the Way, An Autobiography of the Years 1919 to 1939, 1967

    . . . We liked Whittall very much personally, but we came to the conclusion that he was too cultured for us and for the Press. We did not want the Press to become one of those (admirable in their way) 'private' or semi-private Presses the object of which is finely produced books, books which are meant not to be read, but to be looked at. We were interested primarily in the immaterial inside of a book, what the author had to say and how he said it . . .

From Virginia Woolf's diary   *Wednesday 9 January 1924*

    At this very moment, or fifteen minutes ago, to be precise, I bought the ten years lease of 52 Tavistock Sqre London W.C.1 — I like writing Tavistock. Subject of course to the lease, & to Providence . . . the house is ours; & the basement, & the billiard room, with the rock garden on top, & the view of the square in front & the desolated buildings behind, & Southampton Row, & the whole of London . . . music, talk, friendship, city views, books, publishing, something central & inexplicable, all this is now within my reach. So I ought to be grateful to Richmond & Hogarth, & indeed, whether it's my invincible optimism or not, I am grateful . . . Moreover, nowhere else could we have started the Hogarth Press, whose very awkward beginning had rise in this very room, on this very green carpet . . .

Leonard Woolf, Downhill All the Way, An Autobiography of the Years 1919 to 1939, *1967*

 . . . The Hogarth Press was from 1924 to 1939 . . . an extremely efficient publishing business, though its methods were in most ways unorthodox. The business side during those years was managed by me and the succession of young men. The first young man to enter and leave the basement in Tavistock Square — and by no means the least brilliant — was G. W. H. Rylands, universally known as Dadie. We were aiming very high when we took Dadie into the Press and began to turn him into a publisher. Not unnaturally he did not stay long in the basement. When he came to us he was only 22; a scholar of Eton and King's, he had just taken a degree and had written a fellowship dissertation. It was from the first understood that, if he got his fellowship at King's, we should lose him, for he would return to Cambridge to become a don. We treated him rather badly, for almost at once we went off for a week or two, leaving him alone in charge of the Press . . .

From Virginia Woolf's diary   *Monday 15 October 1923*

 . . . This young man [Dadie] with hair like the husk of corn, says he wishes to devote his life to the Hogarth Press, & is writing a letter to that effect to Leonard. This will begin in June. He shall be a partner, & take over the work; & we shall supervise, & by degrees it will become more & more important, & we shall be the benefactors of our age; & have a shop, & enjoy the society of the young, & rummage & splash in the great bran pie, & so never, never stop working with brains or fingers or toes till our limbs fly asunder & the heart sprays off into dust . . .

Leonard Woolf, Downhill All the Way, An Autobiography of the Years 1919 to 1939, *1967*

 . . . Dadie was followed by Angus Davidson, who stayed with us from 1924 to 1929; he is now very well known as a translator of Italian books. He was followed by a very young man, Richard Kennedy . . . In 1931 he left us and John Lehmann entered the Press. His appearance on the scene was to have a considerable effect upon the Press and its fortunes. Unlike the other young men, he took publishing very seriously and became a highly efficient professional publisher . . . Poor John, like Dadie a product of Eton and Cambridge, only 24 years old when he came to us, was put into a small, dark basement room, from which he was expected, under my supervision, to 'manage' the publication of 22 books to be published by us in the spring of 1931. These 22 books included Vita's [Sackville-West] *All Passion Spent* (selling 14,000 copies in the first six months), Virginia's *The Waves* (selling 10,000), a first novel *Saturday Night at the Greyhound* by John Hampson (selling 3,000), and two masterpieces by Rainer Maria Rilke, very difficult publishing propositions 30 years ago, the *Duino Elegies* and *The Notebook of Malte Laurids Brigge*. We published these 22 books — and another 18 in the autumn season of 1931 — with a staff consisting of one traveller and four or five in the office . . .

Leonard Woolf, Downhill All the Way, An Autobiography of the Years 1919 to 1939, *1967*

    . . . In 1929 and 1930 we had published two anthologies, *Cambridge Poetry 1929* and *Cambridge Poetry 1930.* They were anthologies of poetry written, selected, and edited by Cambridge undergraduates. Four of the five Cambridge poets of *New Signatures* — Julian [Bell], John [Lehmann], [Richard] Eberhart, and [William] Empson — were included in these two volumes. We had even penetrated into Oxford, for already in 1929 we had published Cecil Day Lewis's first book of poems, *Transitional Poem.* However, it was not only the emergent poets whom John helped us to keep in touch with. It was through him, via Stephen Spender, that one of the most remarkable and strange of the emergent novelists came to the Hogarth Press, Christopher Isherwood. In 1932 we published *The Memorial,* in some ways his best novel, and in 1935 the brilliant *Mr Norris Changes Trains . . .*

VANESSA BELL
BOOKJACKET OF *THREE GUINEAS,* 1938

From Virginia Woolf's diary   *Friday 3 March* [1939]

   . . . & then off we went to the Polytechnic [London Central School of Arts & Crafts]; & met a little brown faced supple man in corduroys; inspected a wall of illustrations to O[rlando]. & then in came, say 50 art students; blouses, shirts; nimble, young, inquisitive; stood up, & not very nervously spoke, improving, colloquially. Then L. gave his views; as a publisher. And that was a great success — very valuable indeed, said the professor [John Farleigh]; & asked him to start again, which he did. No it wasn't formidable. It was rather cheerful. And free & easy. Better much than Oxford & Cambridge . . .

Hogarth and the War

Leonard Woolf, The Journey not the Arrival Matters, An Autobiography of the Years 1939 to 1969, *1969*

. . . On September 10 [1940] I drove up to London, but found that it was impossible to get into the house in Mecklenburgh Square. The police had cordoned off the Square after evacuating the inhabitants. The neighbourhood had been badly bombed the night before and there was an unexploded bomb in the ground in front of our house. The Hogarth Press had come to a standstill . . . [When the bomb was exploded] our house was in a dreadful state, all the windows blown out, doors hanging on one hinge, and the roof damaged.

VANESSA BELL
BOOKJACKET OF *BETWEEN THE ACTS*, 1941

It was soon still further wrecked by the terrible havoc caused by a land mine which fell at the back, killing several families and blasting all our rooms in reverse direction from the previous bombing.

The Hogarth Press premises in the basement and our flat on the third and fourth floors were uninhabitable. All the windows had been blown out; most of the ceilings had been blown down, so that, in most places, you could stand on the ground floor and look up with uninterrupted view to the roof while sparrows scrabbled about on the joists of what had been a ceiling; bookcases had been blown off the walls and the books lay in enormous mounds on the floors covered with rubble and plaster. In the Press, books, files, paper, the printing-machine and the type were in a horrible grimy mess . . .

In those days the Press printed many of its books with the Garden City Press, Letchworth, Herts., and they nobly came to our rescue. They offered to give us office accommodation within their printing works for our staff if we evacuated them to Letchworth. We accepted gratefully and for the remainder of the war the entire business of The Hogarth Press was carried on from Letchworth . . .

From Virginia Woolf's diary   *Sunday 16 February 1941*

Then Letchworth — the slaves chained to their typewriters, and their drawn set faces, and the machines — the incessant more and more competent machines, folding, pressing, glueing and issuing perfect books. They can stamp cloth to imitate leather. Our Press is up in a glass case. No country to look at. Very long train journeys. Food skimpy. No butter, no jam. Old couples hoarding marmalade and grape nuts on their tables. Conversation half whispered round the lounge fire . . .

Leonard Woolf, The Journey not the Arrival Matters, An Autobiography of the Years 1939 to 1969, *1969*

. . . We were left with very little paper for new writers and new books. We did manage to do something. We cut down our list drastically . . . The standard of what we did publish was, however, pretty high. Between 1939 and 1945 we published Virginia's *Between the Acts*, *A Haunted House*, and *Death of the Moth*. We began the publication of Henry Green's novels with *Party Games* and William Sansom's short stories and novels with *Fireman Flower*. We published books of poetry by Rilke, Robert Graves, Cecil Day Lewis, William Plomer, Hölderlin, Terence Tiller, Vita Sackville-West, Laurie Lee, and R. C. Trevelyan. One of the surprises of the war, which I do not think any publisher foresaw when it broke out, was that, as it dragged on, you could sell anything which could be called a book because it was printed in ink on paper bound in a cover . . . What was even more surprising was that one found that one could sell all one's old stock . . . By the end of the war The Hogarth Press, at any rate, had scraped the last book from the barrel and was left with no unsold stock . . .

In 1967 The Hogarth Press celebrated its fiftieth birthday. It is rather surprising that it should have existed for half a century . . . I was thirty-seven when we printed and published our first book and I was therefore eighty-seven when the Press completed its half-century . . .

OMEGA, CHARLESTON, HOGARTH

DUNCAN GRANT
PORTRAIT OF VANESSA BELL, c.1918

WARDROBE FOR LALLA VANDERVELDE, 1916

ROGER FRY
CIRCULAR TABLE. 1913—14

DUNCAN GRANT
BLUE SHEEP SCREEN, 1912–13

VANESSA BELL
NUDE WITH PAPER POPPIES, 1916

BED FOR LALLA VANDERVELDE — RECUMBENT FEMALE, 1913

DUNCAN GRANT
PORTRAIT OF LYTTON STRACHEY, 1913

DUNCAN GRANT
JULIAN BELL READING, 1930

HENRI DUCET
JULIAN BELL, 1912

DUNCAN GRANT
QUENTIN BELL, 1920

DUNCAN GRANT

FLOWERS IN A GLASS VASE, 1918–19

DUNCAN GRANT
CORNER CUPBOARD, PAINTED FOR ANGUS DAVIDSON, c. 1924

VANESSA BELL

CHARLESTON FARMHOUSE. c.1950

VANESSA BELL

SNOW AT CHARLESTON, VIEW FROM THE STUDIO, c. 1944

DUNCAN GRANT
LESSONS IN THE ORCHARD. 1917

DUNCAN GRANT
THE DOORWAY, 1929

DUNCAN GRANT

LINEN CHEST, c.1916—19

VANESSA BELL
JULIAN BELL AND ROGER FRY PLAYING CHESS, c. 1933

VANESSA BELL

CLIVE BELL AND HIS FAMILY, c.1924

191

FREDERICK ETCHELLS
ENTRY INTO JERUSALEM. 1912

JESSIE ETCHELLS
THREE FIGURES, 1912.

DUNCAN GRANT
CAT. 1932

DUNCAN GRANT
CAT ON A CABBAGE, 1913

VANESSA BELL
FIRESCREEN, 1935

DUNCAN GRANT
WASHSTAND, 1945—50

DUNCAN GRANT
PAINTED LOG BOX, 1916—17

DUNCAN GRANT
MUSIC STOOL, 1924

DUNCAN GRANT

LILYPOND TABLE DESIGN, 1913

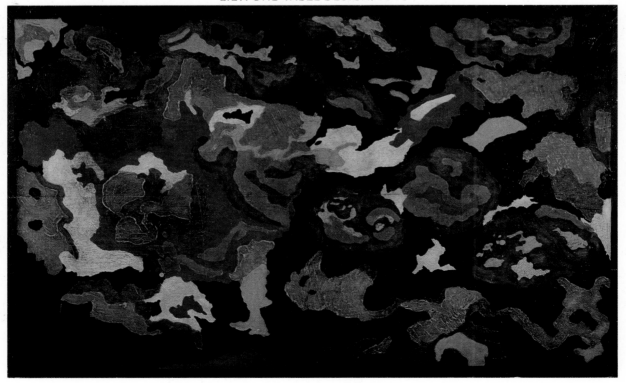

DUNCAN GRANT

LILYPOND TABLE, 1913—14

DUNCAN GRANT
LILYPOND SCREEN, 1914

DUNCAN GRANT

DESIGN FOR TRAY: TROJAN WOMEN. 1913

VANESSA BELL
DESIGN FOR SCREEN, 1913–14

ROGER FRY
DESIGN FOR CADENA CAFÉ RUG, 1914

DUNCAN GRANT
CIRCULAR DESIGN: GIRAFFE, 1913

ROGER FRY
AMENOPHIS III, 1913

VANESSA BELL AND ROGER FRY

PAMELA, 1913

MECHTILDE III, 1913

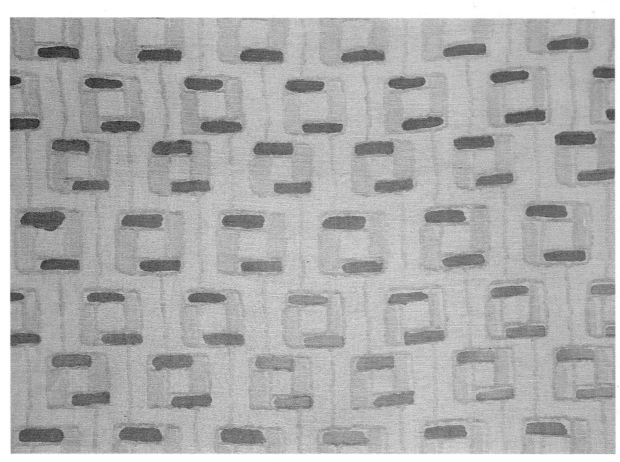

VANESSA BELL

MAUD, 1913

ROGER FRY
AMENOPHIS VI, 1913

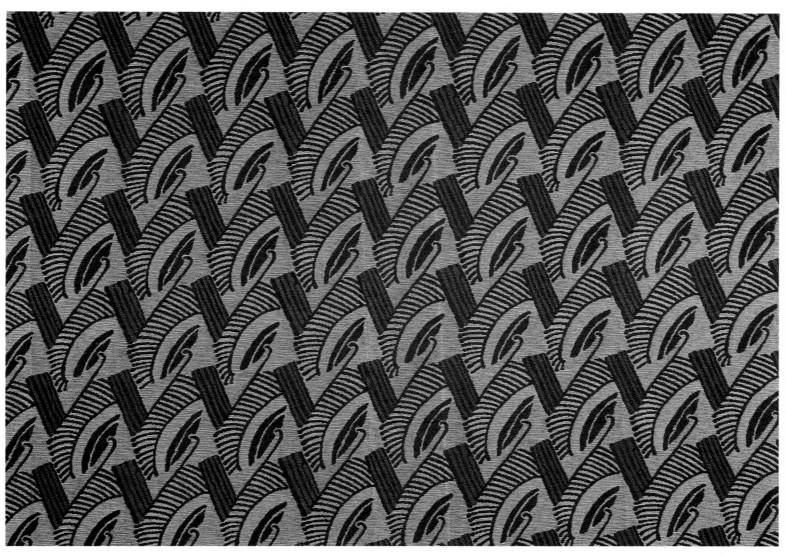

ROGER FRY

CRACOW, 1914

DUNCAN GRANT
STUDY FOR VANESSA BELL RESTING IN A HAMMOCK, 1921—3

DUNCAN GRANT
THE HAMMOCK, 1921–3

ROGER FRY
FARM POND, CHARLESTON, 1918

DUNCAN GRANT
THE BARN BY THE POND, 1925

DUNCAN GRANT
PORTRAIT OF VANESSA BELL IN AN ARMCHAIR, 1915

DUNCAN GRANT
NUDE ON SOFA, c. 1919

DUNCAN GRANT
HELEN ANREP IN CHARLESTON DINING ROOM, 1941

VANESSA BELL
GRACE IN CHARLESTON KITCHEN, 1943

VANESSA BELL
WHITE VI, 1913

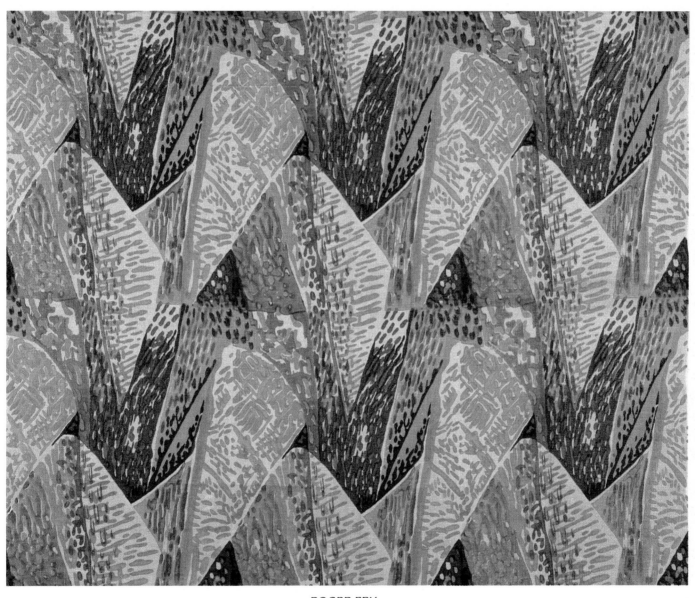

ROGER FRY
MARGERY, 1913

ROGER FRY
PORTRAIT OF NINA HAMNETT, c. 1917

DUNCAN GRANT
GREEN JUG AND BRUSHPOT, 1915–16

ROGER FRY
DESIGN FOR STAINED-GLASS WINDOW, 1915

ROALD KRISTIAN
DESIGN FOR RUG: STALKING BEAR, 1915—16

VANESSA BELL
COUPLE DANCING. 1913

FREDERICK ETCHELLS
DESIGN FOR IDEAL HOME EXHIBITION RUG, 1913

VANESSA BELL
PORTRAIT OF IRIS TREE, 1915

DUNCAN GRANT
PORTRAIT OF IRIS TREE, 1915

DUNCAN GRANT

DESIGN WITH RED FIGURE, c.1913

DUNCAN GRANT
OMEGA SIGNBOARD, 1915

WYNDHAM LEWIS
DESIGN FOR SCREEN – CIRCUS SCENE. 1913

OMEGA CUPBOARD, 1915

ROGER FRY
PROVENCAL VALLEY SCREEN, 1913

ROGER FRY
OMEGA VIRGINAL, 1917—18

DUNCAN GRANT

DECORATION ON A BOOKCASE. c.1925

DUNCAN GRANT
BEDROOM CUPBOARD AT CHARLESTON, c. 1930

DUNCAN GRANT
VANESSA BELL (NÉE STEPHEN), c.1916—17

VANESSA BELL
PORTRAIT OF DAVID GARNETT, c.1916

NINA HAMNETT
SKETCH FOR OMEGA INTERIOR, 1916—17

ROGER FRY
SKETCH FOR INTERIOR FOR LALLA VANDERVELDE, 1916

DUNCAN GRANT

INTERIOR AT GORDON SQUARE. c.1915

VANESSA BELL
PORTRAIT OF HENRI DOUCET, c. 1912

VANESSA BELL
BATHERS SCREEN, 1913

WYNDHAM LEWIS
SELF-PORTRAIT, 1921

DUNCAN GRANT
LANDSCAPE, SUSSEX, 1920

VANESSA BELL
CHARLESTON POND, 1916

ART, DESIGN AND SOCIETY

ROGER FRY AND CLIVE BELL WERE PROLIFIC WRITERS, AND THE FOLLOWING
EXTRACTS FROM THEIR WRITINGS GIVE ONLY AN INDICATION OF THEIR IDEAS AND
THEORIES (WHICH ARE DISCUSSED AT GREATER LENGTH IN THE INTRODUCTION).

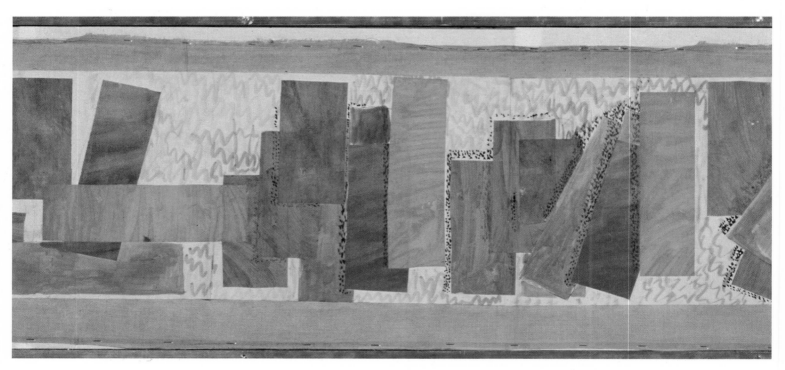

DUNCAN GRANT
ABSTRACT KINETIC PAINTING WITH COLLAGE (detail), 1914

Clive Bell was the more obviously tendentious (and, therefore, more popular) writer: he
presents his ideas with pugnacious panache, and both *Art* (first published in 1914) and
Civilization (1928) were reprinted in inexpensive editions after the Second World War. (*Art*
was also reissued in 1989.) Roger Fry's seminal collection of essays, *Vision and Design*, first
published in 1920, was frequently reprinted, but his later books — including *Transformations*,
a further collection of essays published in 1926 — are less well known.

Fry was the more subtle thinker, and the following extracts, together with those already
quoted, demonstrate the processes by which he achieved his aesthetic, an aesthetic which he
could never quite realize in his paintings. His and Clive Bell's assumptions and attitudes were

similar, a fact which is hardly surprising since they knew each other so well. (Fry, in fact, frequently expressed his irritation at Clive Bell's reiteration of ideas he claimed as his own.) Both were concerned with the nature of aesthetic judgement, with the formal or formalistic elements in art and design, and with what might be described as the spiritual in art; both believed Cézanne to be 'the Christopher Columbus of a new continent of form', and both were preoccupied with an ideal of society, or with the qualities that contribute to an Ideal State.

Clive Bell's *Art* represents the polemic at its most extreme. For him 'the first commandment of art' was 'Thou shall create form', and all his aesthetic judgements related to that premise. His preoccupation with the significance of form, and its power to promote those 'good states of mind' that so preoccupied George Moore and his followers in Cambridge, enables him to dismiss most kinds of narrative painting, notably the work of nineteenth-century British painters as well as that of the Futurists and the Vorticists, who made the fatal mistake of associating art with politics. 'Good as an end in itself' was the only concern of all great art; art did not comment, it did not teach, and its role was neither to depict nor to improve. 'There is no state of mind more excellent or more intense than the state of aesthetic contemplation', wrote Bell; the achievement of this state of mind, however, depended on the sensibilities rather than the education, experience or intellect of the beholder, for 'to appreciate a work of art we need bring with us nothing from life, no knowledge of its ideas and affairs, no familiarity with its emotions'.

This stress on individual interpretation was also fundamental to Fry's philosophy. It is significant, however, that when Fry was campaigning for a Faculty of Art History in Cambridge in 1933 (see page 266), he was pleading for a 'systematic study in which scientific methods will be followed' in furthering the understanding of art. Fry could never and would never abandon his scientific background and training; it was this that led him to place more emphasis on connoisseurship and scholarly enquiry than Clive Bell would ever allow, and it was this that makes him a more challenging critic. There are more complex ambiguities in Fry's thinking: he had absorbed enough of Moore's philosophy still to be preoccupied, in 1933, with art's potential to 'create states of mind'; the aim of research, as far as he was concerned, however, was to concentrate attention on 'what we can get' from works of art rather than on 'what we conceive them to be in themselves'. His preoccupation with the spiritual in art, therefore, like that of Kandinsky twenty years earlier, was perhaps more related to theories of perception and to the psychological impact of form than he himself would have admitted. And he was obviously painfully aware of the dislocation between theory and practice, ideal and achievement in his own painting. His and other 'Bloomsbury' evaluations of the work of Duncan Grant, on the other hand, demonstrate the celebration of the achievements of a painter who confronted theory only to reject it, which makes the dislocation between Bloomsbury theories of art and the painters' practice all the more disconcerting.

Clive Bell on art

Clive Bell, Art, *1914*

In this little book I have tried to develop a complete theory of visual art. I have put forward an hypothesis by reference to which the respectability, though not the validity, of all aesthetic judgements can be tested, in the light of which the history of art from palaeolithic days to the present becomes intelligible, by adopting which we give intellectual backing to an almost universal and immemorial conviction . . .

. . . The starting-point for all systems of aesthetics must be the personal experience of a peculiar emotion. The objects that provoke this emotion we call works of art . . .

. . . There must be some one quality without which a work of art cannot exist; possessing which, in the least degree, no work is altogether worthless. What is this quality? What quality is shared by all objects that provoke our aesthetic emotions? What quality is common to Sta. Sophia and the windows at Chartres, Mexican sculpture, a Persian bowl, Chinese carpets, Giotto's frescoes at Padua, and the masterpieces of Poussin, Piero della Francesca, and Cézanne? Only one answer seems possible — significant form. In each, lines and colours combined in a particular way, certain forms and relations of forms, stir our aesthetic emotions. These relations and combinations of lines and colours, these aesthetically moving forms, I call 'Significant Form'; and 'Significant Form' is the one quality common to all works of visual art . . .

. . . Art is above morals, or, rather, all art is moral because, as I hope to show presently, works of art are immediate means to good. Once we have judged a thing a work of art, we have judged it ethically of the first importance and put it beyond the reach of the moralist . . .

. . . The works of those enterprising young men, the Italian Futurists, are notable examples of descriptive painting. Like the Royal Academicians, they use form, not to provoke aesthetic emotions, but to convey information and ideas. Indeed, the published theories of the Futurists prove that their pictures ought to have nothing whatever to do with art. Their social and political theories are respectable, but I would suggest to young Italian painters that it is possible to become a Futurist in thought and action and yet remain an artist, if one has the luck to be born one. To associate art with politics is always a mistake. Futurist pictures are descriptive because they aim at presenting in line and colour the chaos of the mind at a particular moment; their forms are not intended to promote aesthetic emotion but to convey information . . .

. . . For, to appreciate a work of art we need bring with us nothing from life, no knowledge of its ideas and affairs, no familiarity with its emotions . . .

. . . The fact that significant form was the only common quality in the works that moved me, and that in the works that moved me most and seemed most to move the most sensitive people — in primitive art, that is to say — it was almost the only quality, had led me to my hypothesis before ever I became familiar with the works of Cézanne and his followers. Cézanne carried me off my feet before ever I noticed that his strongest characteristic was an insistence on the supremacy of significant form . . .

. . . To appreciate fully a work of art we require nothing but sensibility. To those that can hear Art speaks for itself: facts and dates do not; to make bricks of such stuff one must glean the uplands and hollows for tags of auxiliary information and suggestion; and the history of art is no exception to the rule. To appreciate a man's art I need know nothing whatever about the artist; I can say whether this picture is better than that without the help of history.

. . . The Pre-Raffaelite method is at best symbolism, at worst pure silliness. Had the Pre-Raffaelites been blessed with profoundly imaginative minds they might have recaptured the spirit of the Middle Ages instead of imitating its least significant manifestations. But had they been great artists they would not have wished to recapture anything. They would have invented forms for themselves or derived them from their surroundings, just as the mediaeval artists did. Great artists never look back . . .

. . . What the future will owe to Cézanne we cannot guess: what contemporary art owes to him it would be hard to compute. Without him the artists of genius and talent who to-day delight us with the significance and originality of their work might have remained port-bound for ever, ill-discerning their objective, wanting chart, rudder, and compass. Cézanne is the Christopher Columbus of a new continent of form . . .

Clive Bell on painters and painting

Clive Bell, 'Since Cézanne', 1922

. . . Paris was the centre of the [Post-Impressionist] movement: from Paris, therefore, I set out. There the movement originated, there it thrives and develops, and there it can best be seen and understood. Ever since the end of the seventeenth century France has taken the lead in the visual arts, and ever since the early part of the nineteenth Paris has been the artistic capital of Europe . . .

. . . To the young painters of 1904, or thereabouts, Cézanne came as the liberator: he it was who had freed painting from a mass of conventions which, useful once, had grown old and stiff and were now no more than so many impediments to expression. To most of them his chief importance — as an influence, of course — was that he had removed all unnecessary barriers between what they felt and its realization in form. It was his directness that was thrilling. But to an important minority the distortions and simplifications — the reduction of natural forms to spheres, cylinders, cones, etc. — which Cézanne had used as means were held to be in themselves of consequence because capable of fruitful development. From them it was found possible to deduce a theory of art — a complete aesthetic even . . .

CHARLESTON GROUP, 1930

. . . Modigliani owed something to Cézanne and a great deal to Picasso: he was no doctrinaire: towards the end he became the slave of a formula of his own devising — but that is another matter. Modigliani had an intense but narrow sensibility, his music is all on one string: he had a characteristically Italian gift for drawing beautifully with ease: and I think he had not much else . . . A minor artist, surely . . .

. . . Although [Seurat] died as long ago as 1891 his importance has not yet been fully realized, his discoveries have not been fully exploited, nor yet has his extraordinary genius received adequate recognition. Seurat may be the Giorgione of the movement. Working in isolation and dying young, he is known to us only by a few pictures which reveal unmistakable and mysterious genius; but I should not be surprised if from the next generation he were to receive honours equal almost to those paid Cézanne . . .

. . . The brave *douanier* [Henri Rousseau] was hardly master enough to have great and enduring influence; nevertheless, the sincerity of his vision and directness of his method reinforced and even added to one part of the lesson taught by Cézanne: also, it was he who — by his pictures, not by doctrine of course — sent the pick of the young generation to look at the primitives. Such as it was, his influence was a genuinely plastic one, which is more, I think, than can be said for that of Gauguin or of Van Gogh. The former seemed wildly exciting for a moment, partly because he flattened out his forms, designed in two dimensions, and painted without chiaroscuro in pure colours, but even more because he had very much the air of a rebel. 'Il nous faut les barbares,' said André Gide; 'il nous faut les barbares,' said we all. Well, here was someone who had gone to live with them, and sent home thrilling, and often very beautiful, pictures which could, if one chose, be taken as challenges to European civilization. To a considerable extent the influence of Gauguin was literary, and therefore in the long run negligible. It is a mistake on that account to suppose — as many seem inclined to do — that Gauguin was not a fine painter.

Van Gogh was a fine painter, too; but his influence, like that of Gauguin, has proved nugatory — a fact which detracts nothing from the merit of his work. He was fitted by his admirers into current social and political tendencies ... Van Gogh was a preacher, and too often his delicious and sensitive works of art are smeared over, to their detriment, with tendencious propaganda. At his best, however, he is a very great impressionist — a neo-impressionist, or expressionist if you like — but I should say an impressionist much influenced and much to the good, as was Gauguin, by acquaintance with Cézanne in his last and most instructive phase. Indeed, it is clear that Gauguin and Van Gogh would not have come near achieving what they did achieve — achieved, mind you, as genuine painters — had they not been amongst the first to realize and make use of that bewildering revelation which is the art of Cézanne ...

... Picasso stands apart: he is the inventor [of Cubism] and most eminent exponent, yet I refuse to call him Cubist because he is so many other things. Braque, who at present confines himself to abstractions, and to taste and sensibility adds creative power, is to my mind the best of the bunch: while Léger, Gris, Gleizes, and Metzinger are four painters who, if they did not limit themselves to a means of expression which to most people is still perplexing, if not disagreeable, would be universally acclaimed for what they are — four exceptionally inventive artists, each possessing his own peculiar and precious sense of colour and design ...

... Marie Laurencin's painting is adorable; we can never like her enough for liking her own femininity so well, and for showing all her charming talent instead of smothering it in an effort to paint like a man; but she is not a great artist — she is not even the best woman painter alive. She is barely as good as Dufy (a contemporary of Picasso unless I mistake, but for many years known rather as a decorator and illustrator than a painter in oils) who, while he confined himself to designing for the upholsterers and making 'images,' was very good indeed. His oil-paintings are another matter. Dufy has a formula for making pictures; he has a *clichè* for a tree, a house, a chimney, even for the smoke coming out of a chimney. In this way he can be sure of producing a pretty article, and, what is more, an article the public likes ...

... The French know enough of Vorticism to know that it is a provincial and utterly insignificant contrivance which has borrowed what it could from Cubism and Futurism and added nothing to either ... Let us hope better of the new generation — recent exhibitions afford some excuse — a generation which, if reactionarily inclined, can always take [Wilson] Steer for a model, or, if disposed to keep abreast of the times and share in the heritage of Cézanne as well as that of Constable, can draw courage from the fact that there is, after all,

.one English painter — Duncan Grant — who takes honourable rank beside the best of his contemporaries . . .

Clive Bell on sculpture and sculptors

Clive Bell, Since Cézanne, *1922*

. . . Aristide Maillol is so obviously the best sculptor alive that to people familiar with his work there is something comic about those discussions in which are canvassed the claims of Mestrovic and Epstein, Archipenko and Bourdelle. These have their merits; but Maillol is a great artist. He works in the classical tradition, modified by Cézanne, thanks largely to whom, I imagine, he has freed himself from the impressionism — the tiresome agitation and emphasis — of Rodin . . .

. . . At home we have Epstein and Dobson; both have been through the stern school of abstract construction, and Epstein has emerged the most brilliant *pasticheur* alive. Brancuzi (a Bohemian) is, I should say, by temperament more Fauve than Doctrinaire. Older than most of Cézanne's descendants, he has nevertheless been profoundly influenced by the master; but the delicacy of his touch, which gives sometimes to his modelling almost the quality of Wei sculpture, he learnt from no one — such things not being taught. Gaudier Brzcska (sic), a young French sculptor of considerable promise, was killed in the early months of the war. He had been living in England, where his work, probably on account of its manifest superiority to most of what was seen near it, gained an exaggerated reputation . . .

Clive Bell, 'Negro Sculpture', essay in Since Cézanne, 1922

. . . Exquisiteness of quality is its [negro sculpture's — see also page 261] most attractive characteristic. Touch one of these African figures and it will remind you of the rarest Chinese porcelain. What delicacy in the artist's sense of relief and modelling is here implied! What tireless industry and patience! Run your hand over a limb, or a torso, or, better still, over some wooden vessel; there is no flaw, no break in the continuity of the surface; the thing is alive from end to end. And this extraordinary sense of quality seems to be universal amongst them. I think I never saw a genuine nigger object that was vulgar — except, of course, things made quite recently under European direction . . .

. . . At the root of this lack of artistic self-consciousness lies the defeat which accounts for the essential inferiority of Negro to the very greatest art. Savages lack self-consciousness and the critical sense because they lack intelligence. And because they lack intelligence they are incapable of profound conceptions. Beauty, taste, quality, and skill, all are here; but profundity of vision is not . . .

. . . I have seen an Oxfordshire labourer work himself beautifully a handle for his hoe, in the true spirit of a savage and an artist, admiring and envying all the time the lifeless

machine-made article hanging, out of his reach, in the village shop. The savage gift is precarious because it is unconscious. Once let the black or the peasant become acquainted with the showy utensils of industrialism, or with cheap, realistic painting and sculpture, and, having no critical sense wherewith to protect himself, he will be bowled over for a certainty. He will admire; he will imitate; he will be undone . . .

Clive Bell on arts and crafts

Clive Bell, Art, *1914*

. . . Do not encourage them [your children] to join guilds of art and crafts, where, though they may learn a craft, they will lose their sense of art. In those respectable institutions reigns a high conception of sound work and honest workmanship. Alas! why cannot people who set themselves to be sound and honest remember that there are other things in life? The honest craftsmen of the guilds have an ideal which is praiseworthy and practical, which is mediocre and unmagnanimous, which is moral and not artistic. Craftsmen are men of principle, and, like all men of principle, they abandon the habit of thinking and feeling because they find it easier to ask and answer the question, 'Does this square with my principles?' – than to ask and answer the question, 'Do I feel this to be good or true or beautiful?' Therefore, I say, do not encourage a child to take up with the Arts and Crafts. Art is not based on craft, but on sensibility; it does not live by honest labour, but by inspiration . . .

. . . In Monsieur Poiret's *Ecole Martine* scores of young French girls, picked up from the gutter or thereabouts, are at this moment creating forms of surprising charm and originality. That they find delight in their work is not disputed. They copy no master, they follow no tradition: what they owe to the past – and it is much – they have borrowed quite unconsciously with the quality of their bodies and their minds from the history and traditional culture of their race. Their art differs from savage art as a French *midinette* differs from a squaw, but it is as original and vital as the work of savages. It is not great art, it is not profoundly significant, it is often frankly third-rate, but it is genuine; and therefore I rate the artisans of the *Ecole Martine* with the best contemporary painters, not as artists, but as manifestations of the movement . . .

Clive Bell on civilization

Clive Bell, Civilization, *1928*

. . . My notion is that a Sense of Values and Reason Enthroned are the parent qualities of high civilization . . .

. . . People who deliberately sacrificed comfort to beauty — with no practical or superstitious end in view — would appear to me to possess a sense of values. To prefer a liberal to a technical education, an education that teaches how to live rather than one that teaches how to gain, is another manifestation of this highly civilized sense. Reason is to my mind enthroned when there is a prevalent opinion that everything requires, and must ultimately admit of, a rational explanation and justification . . .

. . . Reasonableness and a sense of values were the twin characteristics of Athens in her prime. Sweet reasonableness and appropriate seriousness were, as every schoolboy who begins his education on the classical side is informed, the qualities that distinguished Greek life, thought and art: the one is Reason, sweetened by a Sense of Values, the other a Sense of Values, hardened and pointed by Reason . . .

. . . In a universal Honours List for intellectual and artistic prowess the number of French names would be out of all proportion to the size and wealth of the country. Furthermore, it is this traditional basis that has kept French culture up to a certain level of excellence. France has never been without standards. Therefore it has been to France that the rest of Europe has always looked for some measure of fine thinking, delicate feeling, and general amenity . . .

. . . He who possesses a sense of values cannot be a Philistine; he will value art and thought and knowledge for their own sakes, not for their possible utility . . .

. . . The civilized man desires an education which shall be as direct a means as possible to what alone is good as an end. He cultivates his powers of thinking and feeling, pursues truth and acquires knowledge, not for any practical value that these may possess, but for themselves . . .

. . . Anyone who realizes that the sole good as an end is a good state of mind, and that there are no grounds for supposing that such a thing as a collective mind exists, will naturally set store by the individual in whom alone absolute good is to be found . . .

. . . From these primary qualities, Reasonableness and a Sense of Values, may spring a host of secondaries: a taste for truth and beauty, tolerance, intellectual honesty, fastidiousness, a sense of humour, good manners, curiosity, a dislike of vulgarity, brutality, and over-emphasis, freedom from superstition and prudery, a fearless acceptance of the good things of life, a desire for complete self-expression and for a liberal education, a contempt for utilitarianism and philistinism, in two words — sweetness and light . . .

. . . But to live a highly civilized life a man must be free from material cares: he must have food, warmth, shelter, elbow-room, leisure and liberty . . .

. . . Civilization requires the existence of a leisured class, and a leisured class requires the existence of slaves — of people, I mean, who give some part of their surplus time and energy to the support of others. If you feel that such inequality is intolerable, have the courage to admit that you can dispense with civilization and that equality, not good, is what you want. Complete human equality is compatible only with complete savagery . . .

. . . As a means to good and a means to civility a leisured class is essential . . .

. . . Civilization is not incompatible with socialism: a socialist state that wished to be civilized would support an idle class as a means to good just as it would support schools and laboratories. The only question would be how that class should be chosen. At present it is chosen by inheritance, a grossly extravagant system. There is no reason for supposing that the children of rich parents will be exceptionally intelligent and sensitive; and, in effect, the proportion of the existing leisured class which could be described as 'highly civilized' is absurdly small . . .

. . . What, then, is there to prevent a modern society becoming civilized? The answer comes pat. Athens was possible because most Athenians wished to be civilized. Not only the leisured class, but artisans and operatives too, desired 'the good life'. In England we still have the unearned income to support a huge leisured class; the producers, guided by civilized thinkers, have conquered for themselves a fair measure of security and ease; but of what should be the civilizing minority the majority prefers to barbarize itself by lucrative soul-destroying labour and coarse pleasures, while the artisans and operatives devote their newly acquired means to imitating them . . .

. . . In contemporary England, though some thousands I doubt not are as highly civilized as any that ever lived, the group is too small to form that operative nucleus which converts a passive culture into a civilizing force. And the few grow less. The spirit of the age is against them, against them the gospel of work and the notion that men came into the world to make money, play games, go to picture-palaces and race-meetings, drive cars, and beget children. This is the creed of the producers. Those who hold it have no use for economically unproductive work and subtle, difficult pleasures. Those who hold it have no will to civilization. But they have power . . .

Roger Fry: theory and practice

Roger Fry to Hubert Waley   *Durbins, 26 August 1915*

        I think Art is like religion; I'm not at all sure it isn't the same thing or rather an outcome of the same emotion — the emotion of the universal. Anyhow, I think religion ought not to be mixed with morals or treated as subservient to them, and similarly Art. I'm sure that morals are part of the mechanism of life. You can think of an amoral world. Indeed, I suppose no Paradise would be much good unless morals were left at the door, i.e. ethics are not an end in themselves, whereas the emotions of religion and aesthetics are ends in themselves; we should want to go on having them long after the idea of duty has ceased to have any meaning.

It's something like that, I think, that makes me say Art doesn't begin until you've got past the stage of ethics. Ethics is a balance of conflicting claims, Art is a free expression . . .

Roger Fry to Sir Claude Phillips   *33 Fitzroy Square, 17 November 1915*

. . . Yes, I know I'm too intellectual in my art. I don't *elect* not to be spontaneous. I try all ways I can to tap that side of me, I mean the instinctive and subconscious but I have undoubtedly a damned active mind which often 'butts in' when it isn't wanted. I do however prevent my intellect from ever limiting the outlets of my sensibility — hence the, to me, desolating variety of my work . . .

Roger Fry to Marie Mauron   *7 Dalmeny Avenue, 20 June 1920*

. . . My philosophy has been somewhat tried by my exhibition [at The Independent Gallery] here in London. I have worked like a nigger to arrange it well; in fact, I am very pleased with the general appearance. The few people with some feeling for art recognized that I had never done so well, indeed that it was a fairly important manifestation of the classical idea in art. But I have offended English snobbism. My painting is not sufficiently accentuated; there's nothing fashionable in it. There's no formula one can recognize at once. Finally there's nothing to excite the idle gaze of those in search of distraction. Result a complete fiasco. One single little picture and five studies sold, not enough to pay for the canvases, to say nothing of the colours and the frames . . . That is the result of my last effort — really my last, since henceforth I shall shut up shop. I shall not exhibit any more. I shall go on painting and when my canvases are dry I shall roll them up . . .

Roger Fry to Marie Mauron   *Begun in London, God knows when finished*
                                               Hôtel de Londres, Paris VI, 12 April 1922

. . . So here I am in Paris and in a giddier whirl even than in London. London, in truth, is the calm of death compared to Paris . . . Here and there a pure spirit, uncalculating, unenvious, of such is the good Rumanian sculptor Brancusi who lives apart in a vast studio where great blocks of stone and tree trunks lie around from which he evolves one by one his abstract but vital forms. One has the impression of a holy man — a man of the Middle Ages, gentle, tender and thoughtful. How intense and artistic life is here . . .

Roger Fry to Robert Bridges   *7 Dalmeny Avenue, 23 January 1924*

. . . I am delighted to have your criticisms of my book [*Vision and Design*] . . . First of all, my attempts at aesthetic . . . are much more empirical and less philosophical than your criticisms. I very early became convinced that our emotions before works of art were of many kinds and that we failed as a rule to distinguish the nature of the mixture and I set to work by introspection to discover what the different elements of these compound emotions might be and try to get at the most constant unchanging and therefore, I supposed, fundamental emotion. I found that this 'constant' had to do always with the contemplation of form (of course colour is in this sense part of artistic form). It also seemed to me that the emotions resulting from the contemplation of form were more universal (less particularized and coloured by the individual history), more profound and more significant spiritually than any of the emotions which had to do with life . . . I therefore assume that the contemplation of form is a peculiarly important spiritual exercise . . . My analysis of form — lines, sequences, rhythms, etc. — are merely aids for the uninitiated to attain to the contemplation of form: they do not explain. But agreeing that aesthetic apprehension is a pre-eminently spiritual function does not imply for me any connection with morals . . .

Roger Fry to Margery Fry   *Souillac, Lot, 19 July 1924*

My painting seems to be changing completely — I can't help it — I think in the main I'm getting far more colour and a more downright direct method. I think you'll like it and I think they're more unpoetical than ever and I shall not be surprised if they disgust the British public more than ever. But I feel a new sense of power and ease . . .

Roger Fry to Helen Anrep   *Paris, 1 May 1925*

. . . I went yesterday under guidance of [Jacques] Viot, the young *avant-avant-garde* poet, to see the works of the two great Sure-realist painters Miró and Masson. It's the revenge of Germany that has fallen on France — ideography, symbolism, expressionism and all the possibilities of exploiting the public that these bring.

They all worship Paul Klee, a bloody German who does things like this: [ ] only they go of course rather further and occasionally with Allo or HO . . .!! across the canvas and whenever they get intelligible it's fugal variations on cocks and cunts or a little ebullition in a corner of women's breasts cut off and similar delicacies! Masson has also rediscovered for himself the vermicule flaccidities of art nouveau . . . Of course they have some talent but precious little I think, and know that the only safe way is to recommend it by this sort of rubbish . . .

Roger Fry to Helen Anrep   *Hôtel de Londres, Paris, 1 October 1926*

. . . I want to say a very difficult thing . . . My passion for Vanessa was the intensest thing in my life; it's impossible that that should be repeated, but you are infinitely better as my wife than she would have been. You fit in with my spiritual vagabondage, if you understand what I mean — my want of concentration; she is so intense, so concentrated and in a way so narrow in her vision, whereas my insatiable curiosity devours everything. It makes me inefficient and makes me arrive very slowly at any real result, but it's rich and full and your spirit is like that . . .

Roger Fry to Lytton Strachey   *48 Bernard Street, 2 April 1927*

. . . As to Ruskin, what shall I say? I am very much pleased at your thinking of me, but I'm too overcrowded in this house to be able to keep such a mass of incontinent verbiage. It made me wonder what kind of an animal I was at sixteen when I read it with passionate interest, for now it seems to me to be the maundering of a very foolish man who was too lazy to think and too credulous to doubt the value of his mental overflow — rather like those Freudian children who preserve their excreta. It makes Proust a greater mystery than ever. What did he make of it when he spent two years, or was it three, on the study of Ruskin? So I think you'd better keep the stones [*Stones of Venice*] . . .

Roger Fry to Margery Fry   *Baylham, Nr. Ipswich, Christmas Day, 1931*

. . . My lectures have, I don't know why, been rather a big effort. I took in so much that I had to work all the week in between the usual interruptions and the perpetual ringing of the telephone. Then I suddenly realized I had to broadcast on the French show [at the Royal Academy] on Tuesday. On Sunday I got in to the half-hung show and made notes — I had to have my article for the *Listener* ready Monday morning and I then heard that I had to talk for half an hour instead of the usual twenty minutes, so that I only finished writing it the moment I had to go off and deliver it. It's been hectic . . .

Roger Fry to Charles Mauron   *48 Bernard Street, 10 September 1932*

. . . I find myself more and more in the mood of some quite unfashionable Schools such as the Dutch landscapists of the seventeenth century. I have entirely ceased to belong to my age and I find myself more and more disappointed by the academic results of the Cubists and others — ultimately the *avant-gardisme* seems to me more and more nugatory . . .

Roger Fry to Margery Fry   *Almeria, 18 March 1933*

. . . You see Cambridge has wangled the Slade [Fry was appointed to the Slade Professorship at Cambridge in 1933] for me. It really is rather nice of them. It's the old story of the worship of the aged. I'm almost a British institution. We've got some lovely pottery here — so jolly and so cheap that we have bought a wooden trunk covered with ornamental tinwork (the fashion here) and filled it with them to send by sea. I hope they'll arrive all right; there are some for you in the lot . . .

Roger Fry to Gerald Brenan   *48 Bernard Street, 27 January 1934*

My lectures [on the British exhibition at the Royal Academy] were rather dramatic. I fear that I did not satisfy the Custard Islanders' expectations — I said it would be absurd to maintain that ours was one of the great arts of the world, etc., but that it had its own particular qualities which were well worth understanding. However, Sir William Llewellyn, P.R.A., recomforted them afterwards by saying 'When we think of how many British pictures of great value there are not only in the National Gallery but in the Tate and South Kensington Museum and how many in private houses not only in England and Scotland but also in Ireland (cheers) we cannot doubt that British Art has done an incomparable service to mankind': loud cheers and collapse of poor lecturer under pressure of public opinion. I really enjoyed it immensely and in the second lecture gave them a little sermon on the need for a more critical attitude . . .

P.S. After all, England's one of the few places where an art critic could speak severely of great names. In Germany to doubt that Dürer is a supreme master would mean a painful death.

Roger Fry: art and the state

Roger Fry, 'An Essay on Negro Sculpture', Vision and Design, 1920
     . . . Without ever attaining anything like representational accuracy they [negro sculptors] have complete freedom. The sculptors seem to have no difficulty in getting away from the two-dimensional plane. The neck and the torso are conceived as cylinders, not as masses with a square section. The head is conceived as a pear-shaped mass. It is conceived as a single whole, not arrived at by approach from the mask, as with almost all primitive European art. The mask itself is conceived as a concave plane cut out of this otherwise perfectly unified mass . . .

. . . It is curious that a people who produced such great artists did not produce also a culture in our sense of the word. This shows that two factors are necessary to produce the cultures which distinguish civilized peoples. There must be, of course, the creative artist, but there must also be the power of conscious critical appreciation and comparison. If we imagined such an apparatus of critical appreciation as the Chinese have possessed from the earliest times applied to this negro art, we should have no difficulty in recognizing its singular beauty. We should never have been tempted to regard it as savage or unrefined. It is for want of a conscious critical sense and the intellectual powers of comparison and classification that the negro has failed to create one of the great cultures of the world, and not from any lack of the creative aesthetic impulse, nor from lack of the most exquisite sensibility and the finest taste. No doubt, also, the lack of such a critical standard to support him leaves the artist much more at the mercy of any outside influence. It is likely enough that the negro artist, although capable of such profound imaginative understanding of form, would accept our cheapest illusionist art with humble enthusiasm . . .

Roger Fry, 'El Greco', Vision and Design, 1920
     . . . It is curious, therefore, that modern artists should be able to look back with almost equal reverence to Poussin and to El Greco. In part, this is due to Cézanne's influence, for, from one point of view, his art may be regarded as a synthesis of these two apparently adverse conceptions of design. For Cézanne consciously studied both, taking from Poussin his discretion and the subtlety of his rhythm, and from El Greco his great discovery of the permeation of every part of the design with a uniform and continuous plastic theme. The

likeness is indeed sometimes startling. One of the greatest critics of our time, von Tschudi — of Swiss origin, I hasten to add, and an enemy of the Kaiser — was showing me El Greco's 'Laocoon', which he had just bought for Munich, when he whispered to me, as being too dangerous a doctrine to be spoken aloud even in his private room, 'Do you know why we admire El Greco's handling so much? Because it reminds us of Cézanne' . . .

Roger Fry, Art and Commerce, *1926*

. . . It would be untrue to say that machinery is fatal to the work of art. Its effect is to substitute an ideal exactitude for a felt approximation: wherever the machine enters, the nervous tremor of the creator disappears . . .

Roger Fry: art and the State

Roger Fry, 'Art and the State', Transformations, *1926*

. . . There are, I should say, three main branches of public expenditure upon art, and it is possible that each of these would require a separate inquiry. They are (1) the teaching of art in primary and secondary schools and in the Universities, and the more specialized teaching of the Royal College of Art. (2) The employment of artists by the State in the construction and ornamentation of public buildings and public monuments of all kinds. (3) The acquisition, care, and preservation of the artistic treasures of the country. This would include the preservation of ancient monuments throughout the country and the museums and picture galleries belonging to the State.

The teaching of art is by itself a vast and complicated subject, and one of extreme difficulty. I do not know what sums are spent on it by the State and local public bodies acting under State supervision, but in the aggregate they must be very large, and yet there are not a few people who have grave doubts whether any result is produced comparable to this expenditure. It is certain that the positive results are neither brilliant nor encouraging. It is even uncertain whether artistic progress might not be more rapid were the whole of this teaching abandoned. It is fairly certain, for instance, that in the arts of applied design we find ourselves in a backward position as compared, say, with France, and perhaps with other countries, and yet there is reason to think that the people of England have greater aptitudes for art than have ever been realized . . .

. . . The question of the amount the nation spends on museums and galleries would naturally come up for inquiry, and here I can hardly doubt that some of the money which perhaps ought to be saved in other branches of expenditure would be well spent upon this — for in no other direction of its artistic enterprise are results of such value for the general education of the people, produced at so small an outlay as in this. It will, I suspect, be found that as compared with similar institutions in some other countries our museums are starved . . .

... What I believe is of the utmost importance is a clearer recognition of the profession of the — and here the tell-tale fact obtrudes itself that we have no English word for it — the recognition of the — one has finally to fall back in desperation on the German — the *Kunstforscher*. It should be realized that the intelligent understanding of the artistic products of mankind is a quite serious profession, and one which requires a very thorough and somewhat special training from comparatively early years. It is a humane study, and one that requires as a basis a knowledge of the humanities, and therefore it could take its place in a liberal education more readily than many subjects which have none the less acquired a status in our Universities. A degree given on such a subject would indeed imply a more liberal education than, let us say, a degree in Brewing. Whilst a great deal of archaeological knowledge would inevitably be acquired in such a course of study, its aim should not be purely archaeological. It should be rather a course of comparative applied esthetics. The idea would be that the student should acquire such a wide knowledge of artistic form as exemplified in all the various known cultures of the world that, when in presence of any new form, he would recognize its kinship and analogies with other forms belonging to different ages and countries ...

... If the study of art-history be carried on as a comparative study of all cultures alike, we get an antidote to the kind of orthodoxies and *a priori* judgements which result from a narrow concentration. The *Kunstforscher* under such conditions attains by another route to something of the freedom of that artist, to whom the object in itself is everything, its historical references of no interest. Now the advantage for art of there being such a body of men with this special but somewhat detached interest in esthetic values is very great. Not only does it mean that the museums would be likely to acquire the most significant objects of any given culture, but these men would exert an influence on public opinion which no one else could. The pure archaeologist is too insensitive to esthetic values, the artist is too closely interested in his own particular type of creative effort. To such a body, if it existed, the State could turn for direction and guidance with at least more prospect of a well-pondered and judicial opinion than to any body of men at present constituted in this country ...

Roger Fry, 'Vincent Van Gogh', Transformations, 1926

        ... What astonishes one most in the series of [Van Gogh's] pictures is not only the rapidity of the work itself but the rapidity of the evolution which he accomplished. His early painting of a 'Pair of Boots' is a still-life study in which the influence of his early Dutch training and his enthusiasm for Israels are still apparent. This belongs to the year 1886. The latest work seen at the Leicester Galleries is the 'Cornfield with Rooks', done at Auvers just before his death in 1890. And the difference of spirit between these two is immense.

In between lies Van Gogh's *Annus mirabilis* 1888, the year of his sojourn in Provence, of his comradeship with Gauguin and his first tragic outbreak. And in that year he had not only to sum up, as it were, all his past endeavour, but to accept and digest the influence of so dominating a character as Gauguin's. We see him in the 'Zouave', frankly accepting Gauguin's oppositions of flat, strongly coloured, lacquer-like masses, but this is the only obvious evidence of Gauguin's effect on Van Gogh's art. The 'Sunflowers', now in the Tate Gallery, is one of the triumphant successes of this year. It has supreme exuberance, vitality, and vehemence of attack, but with no sign of that loss of equilibrium which affects some of the later works. It belongs to a moment of fortunate self-confidence, a moment when the feverish intensity of his emotional reaction to nature put no undue strain upon his powers of realization.

This is a harmony based almost entirely upon yellows. Against a pale, almost lemon, yellow background the heads of the sunflowers show as dusky masses of heavy burnished gold. Yellows indeed, and pure positive chromes at that, take a preponderant place in Van Gogh's colour scheme. Such a use of yellow is rare in European art. It occurs frequently in Italian paintings of the fourteenth century, and then seems almost to disappear from the palette. It was in Van Gogh's case doubtless due to Oriental influence, since it played so large a part in Chinese decorative design of the seventeenth and eighteenth centuries . . .

. . . He returned to a more than primitive simplicity of statement and built his images with almost the schematic bareness of a child's drawing. Within those limits, however, his conviction gave him a masterly precision and sureness of touch.

It was this peculiarity of Van Gogh's genius that made his influence on the next generation so considerable. His power of communication was so great that it was impossible even for the most casual spectator not to be arrested by it. The very fact that it was so elementary gave it an impressive force in a sophisticated society. When Post Impressionism dawned on our astonished world in 1910 it was, I think, Van Gogh who was the most overpowering revelation. Artists in particular felt that here was the authority for altogether new perspectives. His example inspired them to venture upon innumerable experiments, most of which were doomed to failure, but had at least a healthy effect in making new creations seem possible. It relieved artists of the pressure of discouraging pessimism which the criticism of the day imposed on the world as a mark of fastidious good taste. It destroyed in them the prestige of a culture which preached the doctrine that all real works of art were already enshrined in museums, and that the best that could be hoped for from the modern artist was the multiplication of skilful pastiches. Perhaps nothing short of Van Gogh's blatant anarchism in art could have served this end . . .

Roger Fry, 'Culture and Snobbism', Transformations, 1926

. . . The highly organized production on a grand scale of America, with its large wages and high profits, leaves far fewer of those interstices in the social system into which the artist can insert himself, than does a society based on a multiplicity of small and individual producers. Here, indeed, we touch on one of those small accidental factors in social life which may exercise a decisive influence on artistic production. What wonder, then, that periods of artistic creation and impotence are as hard to predict or account for as the weather itself! Hitherto we have not made anything like as strenuous an effort at estimating and calculating these forces and conditions, doubtless because societies always tend to regard their spiritual products as superfluities. And yet there is a certain irony in the fact that every civilization is ultimately judged by what of spiritual value it has contributed to the human patrimony. It is only at each present moment that this appears to be of so little consequence as to be negligible by the governing class . . .

Roger Fry: architectural heresies

Roger Fry, 'Architectural Heresies of a Painter', lecture delivered at the RIBA, 1921

Heresy No. 1   We have substituted for the art of architecture that art of dressing buildings according to the fashion.

Heresy No. 2   This phenomenon is more or less world wide. In the false architecture of modern Europe which results, the English is distinguished by its lack of the sense of scale.

Heresy No. 3   It is sometimes distinguished also by its good taste. Good taste in this sense is a social rather than an aesthetic virtue.

Heresy No. 4   There are two possible kinds of beauty in a building: (1) What I call natural beauty, which is also the beauty of a locomotive or a panther, and this results from the clear expression of function. (2) Aesthetic beauty which results from the clear expression of an idea. We have so arranged that neither of these beauties occur in our buildings.

Heresy No. 5   Aesthetic beauty in a building is essentially the same as that of sculpture. It results from the expression of a plastic idea. There has hardly been an aesthetic architecture in England and there has been even less sculpture.

Heresy No. 6   Our architecture does not express plastic ideas but historico-social ideas.

Heresy No. 7   It is founded on social snobbery.

Heresy No. 8   The vices of modern English architecture have almost always been inherent in the architecture of England. Modern conditions have brought out the crack

Heresy No. 9   Modern conditions and modern science have put into the hands of architects the greatest opportunity in the history of the world. They have missed it completely.

Heresy No. 10   To a great extent this is their fault . . .

. . . Real style is, I take it, the perfect adaptation of the means of expression to the idea. It results from ease of expression. Style, as it is understood in modern architecture, is essentially a social symbolism . . .

. . . Natural beauty results from perfectly adapted mechanism. I cannot altogether explain why this should be, but it does appear so frequently to follow that I think it may almost be taken as a general principle. The curves of a shell which record the continuous growth of the creature have the kind of harmony and general logic that I mean; but I find the same in many machines in which this adaptation to the stress of natural forces has arrived at perfection — in the lines of a man of war, or a racing yacht, or an aeroplane, or a steel bridge . . .

... I have seen photographs of purely utilitarian structures in America, particularly vast grain elevators and storages when you get a series of immense bare cylinders supporting a flat rectangular block which gave me the idea of an essential plastic architecture much more vividly than any modern buildings ...

Roger Fry: art history

Roger Fry, Art History as an Academic Study, inaugural lecture as Slade Professor at Cambridge, 1933
... Perhaps the reason why I hope so much that before long Cambridge may, like London, set up a faculty of Art History ... is that we are still so terribly ignorant, that we have such a crying need for systematic study in which scientific methods will be followed wherever possible, where at all events the scientific attitude may be fostered and the sentimental attitude discouraged ...

... It seems that we must abandon all hope of making aesthetic judgements of universal validity ...

... In trying to show, first that the search for an objective standard of aesthetic values is hopeless and secondly that, could we attain it, the mere *knowledge* of that standard would be entirely useless to us, I have been trying to bring about something like a shift of perspective in our attitude to aesthetic values. If we regard works of art not as isolated static phenomena but as potentialities for evoking states of mind, we shall concentrate our attention rather on what we can get from them than on what we conceive them to be in themselves ...

Duncan Grant reviewed

Clive Bell, Review of Duncan Grant Exhibition, 1920, Since Cézanne, 1922.
... Duncan Grant is the best English painter alive. And how English he is! (British, I should say, for he is a Highlander.) Of course, he has been influenced by Cézanne and the modern Frenchmen. He is of the movement ...

... Duncan Grant's ancestors are Piero della Francesca, Gainsborough, and the Elizabethan poets. There is something Greek about him, too; not the archaeological Greek of Germany, nor yet the Graeco-Roman academicism of France; but rather that romantic, sensuous Hellenism of the English literary tradition ...

... My notion is that Duncan Grant often starts from some mixed motif which, as he labours to reduce it to form and colour, he cuts, chips, and knocks about till you would suppose that he must have quite whittled the alloy away. But the fact is, the very material out of which he builds is coloured in poetry. The thing he has to build is a monument of pure visual art; that is what he plans, designs, elaborates, and finally executes. Only, when he has achieved it we cannot help noticing the colour of the bricks. All notice, and some enjoy, this adscititious literary overtone. Make no mistake, however, the literary element in the art of Duncan Grant is what has been left over, not what has been added . . .

. . . He has sensibility of inspiration, beauty of touch, and poetry; but, controlling these, he has intelligence and artistic integrity. He is extremely English; but he is more of an artist than an Englishman.

Roger Fry, Living Painters: Duncan Grant, *1923*
. . . Artists like Duncan Grant feel most naturally those harmonies which are easy to grasp, which are fluent, persuasive, and can be followed without effort. This is true not only of the quality of Duncan Grant's design, but also of his colour. In his earlier work particularly his colour had a peculiar pellucid clearness and gaiety. Even when he restricted himself, as he often did, to a limited palette of ochres, greys, and dull greens, he was able to make his tones extraordinarily resonant and gay. In his later work an effort to give more plastic density to his forms has led him to complicate his colour schemes, with the result of a more united effect with some loss of purity and resonance . . .

. . . Gifted as he is with a peculiarly delightful rhythmic sense and an exquisite taste in colour, he is peculiarly fitted to apply his talents to decoration. When he was working at the Omega workshops his fellow-artists all recognized the peculiar charm, the unexpected originality, and the rare distinction of his ideas, and I should be inclined to say that some of the designs which he then made for carpets, for marquetry, and for needlework represent the high-water mark of applied design in England. Later on he has occasionally decorated rooms, working in collaboration with Vanessa Bell, and he has, I think, always succeeded in creating a singularly delightful atmosphere in his interiors, by reason of the unexpectedness of his fancy, the gaiety and purity of his colour – which, however, never ceases to be essentially discrete [sic] and sober – and the perfect adaptation of even the oddest inventions to the decorative purposes of the work in hand . . .

. . . It is indeed greatly to be regretted that so rare a talent as Duncan Grant shows for all kinds of decorative design can find so little outlet in our modern life. And in Duncan Grant's case this is peculiarly regrettable, since it is difficult to him to find scope within the limits of the easel picture for his finest gifts. He is, I think, always more inspired by having a problem of adaptation and a theme for development given to him than when he is confronted with the unlimited possibilities of canvas and oils. And, indeed, the tendency of art of the last few years had been unfavourable to him. The effort to create complete and solidly realized constructions in a logically coherent space, which has succeeded of late to the more decorative conception that derived from Gauguin, has, I think, hampered rather than helped his expression. Duncan Grant co-ordinates form more fully on the flat surface than in three

dimensions. He is more plastic when he suggests relief by the quality of his contour than when he tries to realize it in all its complexity, and finally the attempt to realize a completely coherent three-dimensional whole tends to inhibit invention, which can never hope to attain quite the same completeness of realization as the rendering of the thing seen . . .

Raymond Mortimer, 'Duncan Grant', Penguin Modern Painters, 1944

. . . Duncan Grant was just at the right age to get the most advantage from the new movement. For eight years he had been studying the Old Masters and improving his techniques for depicting appearances so that now he could afford to take liberties. (Post-Impressionism has been a temptation and a trap to many apprentice painters: to try to distort before you can represent is like trying to dance before you can walk.) He began a series of paintings that are without a parallel in the history of the British School. A bunch of flowers, a woman in a bath-tub, a lamp on a table, a coster with a greyhound, a group of ballet-dancers, a friend sitting in a garden — anything, indeed, that caught his eye and memory provided a theme upon which he would elaborate a fantasia. The natural forms were wrested into arabesques; the colours were arbitrary or rather chosen merely for the felicity of their interaction; the concern with volume was hardly greater than in Chinese and Sienese painting. At the time these pictures were astonishing, and intensely delightful to the few who were able to accept them. . . .

. . . In 1913 Roger Fry, always indefatigable in enterprise, organized the Omega workshops for the production and sale of applied art. The designs were couched in the idiom of Post-Impressionism, and here for the first time cubism was applied to textiles, noble ancestors, as it were, of the degenerate 'modernist' stuffs that now proliferate. Fry had a particular distaste for the mechanical rigidity of pattern in machine-made goods — a rigidity prized by the 'functionalist' school of modern designers. He insisted, therefore, on the value of the slight irregularities that reveal the hand of the artist even in the repetitions of a formal design. Duncan Grant has a charming 'handwriting' whether he is defining a contour in a nude study or scribbling a border for a book-jacket or a carpet. He may be thought, however, to exaggerate sometimes the irregularities admired by Roger Fry, and also, as it were, to over-punctuate: the tendency to multiply criss-crosses and croquet-hoops round his decorations, to leave not an inch unadorned, is a legacy, I presume, from the Omega workshops . . .

. . . Grant, from the days of the Omega workshops, has remained interested in applied art. The textiles he designed for the firm of Allan Walton I consider the most beautiful printed stuffs I have seen. He has also designed delightful dinner and tea services for Messrs Brain; and he has painted on pots and plates made by Miss Phyllis Keyes. Embroideries of his design, executed with consummate taste by his mother, are masterpieces of contemporary art. But the history of his most important commission is a cautionary tale. In 1935 he was engaged to decorate a large room in SS *Queen Mary*. The scheme included three great painted panels; but when these were completed, Sir Percy Bates, the chairman of the Cunard-White-Star Company, intervened, and refused to have them put up. I see good reasons for this decision.

They would have contrasted violently with the style of decoration in which the rest of the ship was lavishly embellished. Moreover, they would certainly not have appealed to the film-stars, opera-singers, oil-magnates and other Big Business tycoons who before the war were bound to be the most valuable patrons of a luxury liner. It would perhaps have been better if the Company had thought of this before commissioning so distinguished and so inappropriate an artist. The panels have found an honourable home for the present in the canteen of the National Gallery.

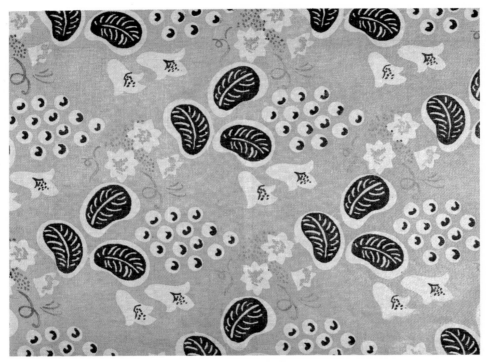

DUNCAN GRANT

GRAPES, 1932

Unluckily a lot of Duncan Grant's decorative work has been destroyed by German bombs. The houses of Miss Sands and Mr and Mrs Woolf were demolished; so was the artist's own studio in Fitzroy Street, with some of his works in it. He has now completed a large wall-painting for the chancel-arch of the parish church of Berwick in Sussex, near his country home, while Vanessa Bell has decorated the sides of the chancel with an Annunciation and a Nativity. She has collaborated with Grant in so many of his decorations that when writing about his work the critic must also consider hers. It is sometimes assumed that she is, as it were, his pupil. Certainly there are conspicuous similarities between Vanessa Bell's work and Duncan Grant's, and often they have painted simultaneously from the same model. Yet it seems to me clear that the influence has been not one-sided but reciprocal. Careful comparison suggests moreover that, though they share many tastes, they are quite unlike in

temperament. Vanessa Bell is, I think, by nature a realist. (Unlike Grant she has a great gift for catching a likeness.) She is altogether a graver, less exuberant, artist; her landscapes and still-lifes bear the signs of careful consideration and are all the better for this. The resemblances between her work and his have, I think, prevented her gifts receiving the full appreciation that they merit. Their virtues seem to me markedly different in character, and each paints best when painting least like the other. The tempo natural to her is *andante*, while his is *allegro* . . .

DUNCAN GRANT
STUDY FOR A POSTER FOR BERWICK CHURCH, 1969

. . . I believe Grant to be conspicuous in the history of the British School alike for his gifts and for the energy and integrity with which these have been cultivated. I hope that after the war public bodies will prove more discriminating than rich men have shown themselves; and that the country of his birth, having at last produced a consummate decorator, will provide him with the opportunities he deserves, and posterity with a legacy of fine visual pleasure.

PART VII

JUDGEMENTS

Quentin Bell, Bloomsbury, *1968*

... I think that Bloomsbury's tolerance was tried fairly high by the younger generation. For we had no hesitation — and that in itself is significant — in telling Old Bloomsbury that it had taken the wrong turning, that it had entirely misjudged the social and political situation before 1914, that it ought to have foreseen the war and that its attitude then had been purely negative. Furthermore we pointed out that it had allowed Post-Impressionism to degenerate into something wholly frivolous and fashionable, that it acquiesced in a social system which it knew to be wrong and allowed itself to become a part of the Establishment. Finally that it failed altogether to see that the one hope of the world, despite all its errors and despite all the civilized squeamishness that it might provoke, was Soviet Russia. Such, very roughly, and with great differences of individual position, was the case that we made against Bloomsbury, and it was argued with increasing tension as the drama of the thirties developed. Bloomsbury was always ready to listen to such opinions and to debate them fairly.

This last paragraph has carried me beyond the twenties and into a period in which Bloomsbury was but a shadow of its former self, even though some of its members still had important tasks to accomplish. The deaths of Lytton Strachey in 1931 and of Roger Fry in 1934 altogether changed the character of the group. The events of the thirties left it without any common doctrine or attitude. As I have said, the 1920s made it and broke it; it was then that it soared, burst in lazy scintillating splendour and slowly expired in still-glowing fragments ...

... Even those who would declare that faith is in some sort a higher thing than reason would, probably, agree that there is a good deal to be said for this view — in theory. The difficulty, as anyone who surveys the world from Birmingham, Alabama to Salisbury, Rhodesia, and back again by way of Saigon, will know is that when it comes to a struggle between reason and violence reason nearly always takes a beating.

And yet this is not the whole picture. Reason does win victories and Bloomsbury has helped to win them. This paradoxically is one of the things that makes us undervalue its achievements. It would be quite easy to compile an anthology of Bloomsbury's pronounce-ments on prudery, sexual persecution and censorship, which would command the assent of nearly all literate people at the present day and would, for that reason, be rather dull; the audacities of one age become the platitudes of the next.

But in its larger effort, the effort to live a life of rational and pacific freedom, to sacrifice the heroic virtues in order to avoid the heroic vices, Bloomsbury was attempting something which, to the next generation, seemed unthinkable. It could only have been thought of by people in a favoured social position at a particularly favourable moment in the history of

England. It could be maintained, but only just maintained, between the years 1914 and 1918 because in that war it was still possible for an intelligent man or woman to be neutral. The advocates of reason, tolerance and scepticism frequently found themselves confronted by individuals who were partly or wholly on the other side . . . But with all of these, as also with a belligerent England, some kind of parley, some kind of communication was possible; between them and Bloomsbury there was not a complete polarity of views. With the advent of Fascism, Bloomsbury was confronted by a quarrel in which, believing what they believed, neutrality was impossible. The old pacifism had become irrelevant and the group as a group ceased to exist.

Angelica Garnett, Deceived with Kindness, *1984*

    . . . To others our narcissism must have been painfully evident, while to ourselves it seemed as though we were exhibiting the purest spirit of objective detachment — in either case it was hardly an atmosphere which welcomed outsiders, and the very fact that we thought of them as such was a betrayal of our attitude. In fact we were almost encouraged to condemn people out of hand as though we had a divine right to judge, and dismiss those who didn't make the grade. We not only got a wicked pleasure from doing it with many of those we called our friends, but also with the dead, artists such as Mendelssohn or the Pre-Raphaelites whom we had decided to despise. I was probably the worst offender, copycatting my elders without their wit, always able to raise a laugh by such means, until one day Bunny, my future husband, said, 'You must stop being so disdainful of those who are unlike yourself.' It was one of those rare occasions when criticism really sinks in, and I *did* stop, as though provided with a pair of brakes . . .

Gerald Brenan, South from Granada, *1957*

    . . . Looking back today it is not, I think, difficult to see that the weakness inherent in the splendid flower of English culture thrown up by 'Bloomsbury' lay in its being so closely attached to a class and mode of life that was dying. Already by 1930 it was pot-bound. Its members were too secure, too happy, too triumphant, too certain of the superiority of their Parnassian philosophy to be able to draw fresh energies from the new and disturbing era that was coming in. They had escaped the shock of the first German War either by being unfit for military service or by joining the ranks of the pacifists, and had not taken warning from the prophets who announced that the snug rationalist world they lived in was seriously threatened. When they should, therefore, have been in their prime, they were on their way to being an anachronism . . . Yet, I imagine, if the cobalt bomb does not obliterate everything, future ages will feel an interest in these people because they stand for something that the world always looks on with nostalgia — an *ancien régime*. They carried the arts of civilized life and friendship to a very high point, and their work reflects this civilization . . .

Leonard Woolf, paper for Memoir Club *(undated)*

    . . . The downfall — I use the word in the sense given to it by the servant class — of Bloomsbury was its intolerance of every one and every thing which was not

all the time amusing. Perhaps that is an exaggeration, but it is true that, just as one hesitated in Moore's rooms at Cambridge to say anything amusing which was not also profound and true, so in Bloomsbury one hesitated to say anything true or profound unless it was also amusing. In my experience what is amusing is very rarely true or profound, and what is true or profound is hardly ever amusing . . .

Leonard Woolf, Downhill All the Way, An Autobiography of the Years 1919 to 1939, *1967*

. . . One afternoon I was planting in the orchard under an apple-tree iris reticulata, those lovely violet flowers which, like the daffodils, 'come before the swallow dares and take the winds of March with beauty'. Suddenly I heard Virginia's voice calling to me from the sitting-room window: 'Hitler is making a speech'. I shouted back: 'I shan't come. I'm planting iris and they will be flowering long after he is dead.' Last March, 21 years after Hitler committed suicide in the bunker, a few of those violet flowers still flowered under the apple-tree in the orchard.

DUNCAN GRANT
VANESSA BELL AT HILTON HALL WITH HER GRANDCHILD WATCHING, date unknown

ART AND DESIGN

ROGER FRY
CLIVE BELL, c.1924

DUNCAN GRANT
HAYSTACK BEFORE TREES, 1940

DUNCAN GRANT
FONTCREUSE, 1934

PLATES III

DUNCAN GRANT
DESIGN FOR RIGHT-HAND PANEL OF EMBROIDERED SCREEN, c. 1930

DUNCAN GRANT
THREE-PANELLED EMBROIDERED SCREEN. c.1930

DUNCAN GRANT
DESIGN FOR FABRIC, 1931

DUNCAN GRANT
QUEEN MARY, 1937

VANESSA BELL
THE COOK, 1948

DUNCAN GRANT
GIRL AT THE PIANO, 1940

VANESSA BELL

INTERIOR WITH HOUSEMAID, 1939

284

VANESSA BELL
THE WEAVER, 1937

VANESSA BELL
CATHEDRAL, LUCCA, 1949

VANESSA BELL
BRIGHTON PIER. 1955

DUNCAN GRANT
VANESSA BELL. 1942

VANESSA BELL
LEONARD WOOLF, 1940

ROGER FRY
BRIDGE OVER ALLIER, c. 1933

VANESSA BELL
INTERIOR WITH DUNCAN GRANT, 1934

DUNCAN GRANT
ANGELICA PLAYING THE VIOLIN, 1934

VANESSA BELL
LADY STRACHEY, 1922

DUNCAN GRANT
SOUTH OF FRANCE, 1922

DUNCAN GRANT
THE ITALIAN HANDKERCHIEF, 1935

DUNCAN GRANT
RECLINING NUDE, c. 1930

DUNCAN GRANT
PORTRAIT OF MISS HOLLAND, c.1937

VANESSA BELL
SELF-PORTRAIT, 1958

DUNCAN GRANT

AUTUMN FLOWERS IN A VASE ON A TABLE, 1964

PLATES III

DUNCAN GRANT

ANGEL STUDIES FOR *CHRIST IN GLORY*, BERWICK CHURCH, 1941–3

DUNCAN GRANT

COMPLETE STUDY FOR *CHRIST IN GLORY*, BERWICK CHURCH, 1941–3

VANESSA BELL

STUDIES FOR BERWICK CHURCH MURALS: *THE ANNUNCIATION* AND *THE BIRTH OF CHRIST*, 1941–3

VANESSA BELL
BERWICK CHURCH MURAL — *THE ANNUNCIATION*, 1941—3

DUNCAN GRANT
BALLET DECORATION, date unknown

VANESSA BELL
BACKDROP DESIGN FOR *HIGH YELLOW*, c.1932

DUNCAN GRANT

THE ENCHANTED GROVE I. date unknown (pre—1924)

DUNCAN GRANT
THE ENCHANTED GROVE II. date unknown (pre—1924)

VANESSA BELL
HENRIETTA GARNETT, 1957

DUNCAN GRANT
VANESSA PAINTING. 1961

DUNCAN GRANT

HAND-PAINTED URN-SHAPED VASE, c.1937

VANESSA BELL

HAND-PAINTED VASE, 1930s

BIOGRAPHIES

The Bloomsbury Group: members, families and associates

CLIVE BELL (1881–1964). Writer and art critic. Son of William Heward Bell, colliery owner and mining engineer. Educated Marlborough and Trinity College, Cambridge. Married Vanessa Stephen, 1907; father of Julian and Quentin Bell.

JULIAN BELL (1908–1937). Writer and poet. Elder son of Clive and Vanessa Bell. Killed while serving as an ambulance driver in the Spanish Civil War.

QUENTIN BELL (1910–   ). Art historian, biographer, painter and potter. Emeritus Professor of the History and Theory of Art, Sussex University. Younger son of Clive and Vanessa Bell.

VANESSA BELL (Nessa) (1879–1961). Painter and designer. Elder daughter of Leslie and Julia Stephen. Married Clive Bell, 1907; mother of Julian, Quentin and Angelica Bell.

GEORGE HERVERT DUCKWORTH (1868–1934). Son of Herbert Duckworth (died 1870) and Julia (née Jackson); brother of Gerald and Stella, and half-brother of Vanessa, Thoby, Virginia and Adrian Stephen.

GERALD DUCKWORTH (1870–1937). Brother of George and Stella; half-brother of the Stephen siblings. Set up his own publishing house, 1898, and published Virginia Woolf's first novel, *The Voyage Out*, in 1915.

STELLA DUCKWORTH (1869–1897). Sister of George and Gerald, and half-sister of the Stephens. Married Jack Hills 1897.

EDWARD MORGAN FORSTER (Morgan) (1879–1970). Novelist and critic. King's College, Cambridge. Apostle. Hon. Fellow, King's College, Cambridge. Novels include *Where Angels Fear to Tread*, *The Longest Journey*, *Howard's End*, and *A Passage to India*.

SIR EDWARD FRY (1827–1918). Eminent Quaker and Judge. Knighted 1877. Married Mariabella (*née* Hodgkin). Father of Portsmouth, Mariabella (Mab), Joan, Margery, Agnes, Roger, Isabel, and Ruth.

JOAN FRY (1862–1955). Active as a Quaker. Kept house for her brother Roger during his wife's illness.

MARGERY FRY (Ha) (1872–1957). Studied at Somerville College, Oxford, and became Principal of Somerville, 1926. Promoted the Howard League for Penal Reform.

ROGER FRY (1866–1934). Painter, writer and art critic. Son of Sir Edward and Lady Mariabella Fry. Educated Clifton College, Bristol, and King's College, Cambridge. Apostle. Married Helen Coombe, 1896; father of Julian and Pamela (Diamand); lived with Helen Anrep from c. 1926.

ANGELICA GARNETT (1918–   ). Writer and painter. Daughter of Vanessa Bell and Duncan Grant. Married David Garnett, 1942.

DAVID GARNETT (Bunny) (1892–1981). Author and publisher. Son of Edward and Constance Garnett; married, first, Rachel (Ray) Marshall (Frances Partridge's sister), 1921; second, Angelica Bell, 1942.

DUNCAN GRANT (1885–1978). Painter and designer; son of Major Bartle and Ethel Grant; cousin of Lytton Strachey. Father of Angelica Garnett.

MARY HUTCHINSON (1899–1977). A cousin of the Stracheys. Married St John Hutchinson; had a long-term love affair with Clive Bell. Patron of Vanessa Bell and Duncan Grant.

JOHN MAYNARD KEYNES (1883–1946). Economist. Educated Eton and King's College, Cambridge. Apostle. Fellow and Bursar of King's College, Cambridge. Wrote the seminal *Economic Consequences of the Peace* (1919) at Charleston. Married Lydia Lopokova, Russian ballerina, 1925. Created Baron Keynes of Tilton, 1942.

DESMOND MACCARTHY (1877–1952). Writer and critic. Educated Trinity College, Cambridge. Apostle. Literary editor of the *New Statesman*, 1920–27; literary critic *The Sunday Times*, 1928–52. Married Mary (Molly) Warre-Cornish, 1906. Knighted 1951.

RAYMOND MORTIMER (1895–1980). Writer and critic. Educated Balliol College, Oxford. Literary editor of the *New Statesman*, 1935–47; wrote for *The Sunday Times* and the *Times Literary Supplement*.

ADRIAN STEPHEN (1883–1948). Doctor and psychoanalyst. Son of Leslie and Julia Stephen; brother of Vanessa, Thoby and Virginia. Married Karin Costelloe, sister of Oliver Strachey's wife Ray; father of Ann and Judith.

LESLIE STEPHEN (1832–1904). Writer, biographer and critic. First editor of the *Dictionary of National Biography*. Married, first, Harriet Thackeray (died 1875); second, Julia Duckworth (née Jackson), 1878; step-father of George, Stella and Gerald Duckworth. Father of Vanessa, Thoby, Virginia and Adrian Stephen.

THOBY STEPHEN (The Goth) (1880–1906). Trinity College, Cambridge. Brother of Vanessa, Virginia and Adrian. Died of typhoid fever following visit to Greece.

JAMES STRACHEY (1887–1967). Educated Trinity College, Cambridge. Apostle. Psychoanalyst; translated edited works of Sigmund Freud, published by the Hogarth Press. Brother of Lytton.

LYTTON STRACHEY (1880–1932). Writer, critic and biographer. Son of Lieut.-Gen. Sir Richard Strachey and Lady Jane Strachey (née Grant). Educated Trinity College, Cambridge, Apostle. Books include *Eminent Victorians* (1918); *Queen Victoria* (1921). Brother of Dorothy, Philippa, Oliver, Pernel, Marjorie and James Strachey.

MARJORIE STRACHEY (Gumbo or Jumbo) (1882–1964). Teacher and writer.

OLIVER STRACHEY (1874–1960) Studied music in Vienna and worked in India. Employed as a code-breaker for the Foreign Office. Married Ray Costelloe (sister of Karin, Adrian Stephen's wife).

PERNEL STRACHEY (1876–1951). Principal of Newnham College, Cambridge.

PHILIPPA STRACHEY (1872–1951). Active in Women's Suffrage Movement. Friend of Roger Fry.

SAXON SYDNEY-TURNER (1880–1962). Trinity College, Cambridge. Civil servant in the Treasury.

LEONARD WOOLF (1880–1969). Writer, political theorist, editor and publisher. Son of Sidney Woolf, Q.C. and Marie (née de Jongh). Trinity College, Cambridge. Apostle. Ceylon Civil Service, 1904–11. Married Virginia Stephen, 1912. They founded The Hogarth Press in 1917. Numerous books include autobiography in 5 volumes.

VIRGINIA WOOLF (1882–1941). Novelist and critic. Daughter of Leslie and Julia Stephen, and sister of Vanessa, Thoby and Adrian. Married Leonard Woolf, 1912. Her novels include: *The Voyage Out* (1915); *Night and Day* (1919); *Mrs Dalloway* (1925); *To the Lighthouse*; (1927); *The Waves* (1931); *Between the Acts* (1941). Her biography of *Roger Fry* was published in 1940. Essays and non-fiction include: *A Room of One's Own* (1929) and *Moments of Being* (1976).

Brief biographies of others mentioned in the text

HELEN ANREP (1885–1965). Wife of Russian sculptor Boris Anrep. Lived with Roger Fry from c. 1926.

C.R. ASHBEE (1863–1943). Architect and designer. King's College, Cambridge (where he met Roger Fry). Founded Guild of Handicraft, 1888.

BARBARA BAGENAL (née Hiles). (1891–1984) Painter. Friend of Clive and Vanessa Bell.

BERNARD BERENSON (1865–1959). Art historian, connoisseur and expert on Italian art. Married Mary Pearsall Smith.

MARY BERENSON (1864–1945). (Mariechen) Married, first, Robert Costelloe (daughters Karin and Ray); second Bernard Berenson.

FRANCIS BIRRELL (Frankie). (1889–1935) Eton and King's College, Cambridge. Critic and biographer. Wrote for the *Nation*.

DAVID BOMBERG (1890–1957). Painter. Founder member of London Group. Briefly associated with Omega Workshops.

EDOUARD AUGUSTE BRÉAL (1869–1941). French painter and writer. Research Fellow, Cambridge, late 1880s, where he met Roger Fry. Friend of Simon and Dorothy Bussy.

GERALD BRENAN (1894–1987). Writer; friend of Virginia and Leonard Woolf, Lytton Strachey, Julian Bell and Roger Fry.

ROBERT BRIDGES (1844–1930). Poet Laureate and author of *The Testament of Beauty*. Friend of Roger Fry.

OSCAR BROWNING (1837–1923). Historian and Fellow of King's College, Cambridge.

DOROTHY BUSSY (née Strachey) (1866–1960). Writer and translator. Friend and translator of André Gide. Author of *Olivia*. Married Simon Bussy.

SIMON BUSSY (1870–1954). Born in Switzerland; studied in Paris, where he met Matisse. Came to England 1901. Involved with New English Art Club. Married Dorothy Strachey, 1903. (They lived for most of the year in Roquebrune, South of France).

EDWARD CARPENTER (1844–1929). Writer and philanthropist. Early influence on Roger Fry.

SIR CASPER PURDON CLARKE (1846–1911). Keeper, Art Collection, Victoria & Albert Museum, London, 1892; Director of the Metropolitan Museum of Art, New York, 1905.

BIOGRAPHIES

HELEN COOMBE Painter: worked for A.H. Mackmurdo's Century Guild before her marriage to Roger Fry in 1896. Son (Julian) born 1901: daughter (Pamela) born 1902. Shortly after her marriage she began to suffer from mental illness.

JACQUES COPEAU (1879–1949). French theatrical producer. Commissioned sets for a production of *Twelfth Night* from Duncan Grant, 1913.

KARIN COSTELLOE (1890–1953). Psychologist. Daughter of Mary Berenson and wife of Adrian Stephen.

SIR AUGUSTUS MOORE DANIEL (1866–1950). Art historian and critic: Trinity College, Cambridge, where he became friendly with Roger Fry. Travelled with Fry to Italy, 1894. Expert on Italian Art. Director of the National Gallery, London, 1929–33.

ANGUS DAVIDSON (1898–1980). Writer and translator. Worked at the Hogarth Press. Friend of Duncan Grant and Vanessa Bell.

ANDRÉ DERAIN (1880–1954). French painter: friend of Roger Fry and Clive Bell.

GOLDSWORTHY LOWES DICKINSON (1862–1932). Historian and philosopher. Fellow of King's College, Cambridge. Friend of Roger Fry.

HENRI DOUCET (1883–1915). French painter and designer. Exhibited in Second Post-Impressionist Exhibition. Associated with Omega Workshops.

HELEN DUDLEY (d. 1914). American: briefly engaged to Bertrand Russell. Painted by Vanessa Bell.

FREDERICK ETCHELLS (1886–1973). Painter and architect. Involved in Borough Polytechnic project, and exhibited in the Second Post-Impressionist Exhibition. Associated with the Omega Workshops: left with Wyndham Lewis. Translated Le Corbusier's *Towards a New Architecture*, 1927. Advised on the Berwick Church project.

JESSIE ETCHELLS (1892–1933). Painter. Sister of Frederick. Included in the Second Post-Impressionist Exhibition. Worked briefly at Omega Workshops.

CHARLES WELLINGTON FURSE (1868–1904). Painter. Member of the New English Art Club.

HENRI GAUDIER-BRZESKA (1891–1915). French sculptor. Moved to London 1911. Founder member of Vorticist Group.

ANDRÉ GIDE (1869–1951). French novelist and critic. Friend of Roger Fry.

WINIFRED GILL (1891–1981). Painter. Associated with the Omega Workshops.

FREDERICK SPENCER GORE (1878–1914). Painter. Member of the New English Art Club. Exhibited at the Second Post-Impressionist Exhibition, 1912. Associated with Wyndham Lewis and the 'Ideal Home Rumpus'.

LADY IAN HAMILTON (1862–1941). Patron of Omega Workshops. (Decorations for her house at 1 Hyde Park Gardens.)

NINA HAMNETT (1890–1956). Painter and writer. Associated with Omega Workshops. Married (briefly) Roald Kristian.

SIR PHILIP HENDY (1900–1980). Former Director of the National Gallery, London.

GLADYS HINES (1888–1959). Painter. Associated with Omega Workshops.

SIR CHARLES HOLMES (1868–1936). Editor of *Burlington Magazine* 1903–9: Director of The National Portrait Gallery, London, 1916–28: Director of the National Gallery, London, 1916–28.

EDWARD MCKNIGHT KAUFFER (1890–1954). Artist and poster designer. Born in America. Came to England 1914. Associated with Omega Workshops.

ROALD KRISTIAN (1893–†). Painter and sculptor: born in Norway and studied in Paris, where he met Nina Hamnett, and married her in London. Associated with Omega Workshops. Deported during First World War.

WILLIAM MACKAY LAFFAN (1848–1909). American journalist and newspaper proprietor. Trustee of the Metropolitan Museum, New York and art advisor to J. Pierpont Morgan.

WALTER LAMB (1882–1961) Classicist and Secretary of the Royal Academy 1931–1951. Brother of Henry, associated with 'Old Bloomsbury'.

HENRY LAMB (1883–1960). Painter. Friend of Lytton Strachey and the Bells.

JOHN LEHMANN (1907–87). Poet, writer and publisher. Worked at The Hogarth Press. Friend of Julian Bell.

PERCY WYNDHAM LEWIS (1884–1957). Painter and writer. Exhibited in Second Post-Impressionist Exhibition. Briefly associated with Omega Workshops. Resigned, along with Frederick Etchells, William Roberts and Edward Wadsworth, following the 'Ideal Home Rumpus'.

ANDRE LHOTE (1885–1962). French painter and writer. Admired by Roger Fry.

JOHN MCTAGGART ELLIS MCTAGGART (1866–1925). Philosopher and lecturer, King's College, Cambridge. At school with Roger Fry: they were close friends for several years.

BIOGRAPHIES

JEAN MARCHAND (1883—1941). French painter admired by the Bloomsbury Group.

CHARLES MAURON (1899—1966). French writer. Friend of Roger Fry.

MARIE MAURON (1898—†). French writer. Friend and confidante of Roger Fry.

JOHN HENRY MIDDLETON (1846—96). Slade Professor of Fine Art, Cambridge; Director of Fitzwilliam Museum, Cambridge.

GEORGE EDWARD MOORE (1873—1958). Philosopher; Professor of Philosophy, University of Cambridge, 1925—39. His ideals, and his book, *Principia Ethica* (1903), had a great influence on the Bloomsbury circle.

JOHN PIERPONT MORGAN (1873—1913). Banker, entrepreneur and art collector. Millionaire. Benefactor of Metropolitan Museum, New York. Patron, for a brief time, of Roger Fry.

LADY OTTOLINE MORRELL (1873—1938). Society hostess; lived in Bloomsbury and Garsington Manor, Oxford. Patron of avant-garde artists and writers.

PAUL NASH (1889—1946). Painter, designer, illustrator. Briefly associated with Omega Workshops.

H.T.J. NORTON (1886—1937). Mathematician. Trinity College, Cambridge. Apostle. Friend of many of the founder members of the Bloomsbury Group.

FRANCES PARTRIDGE (NÉE MARSHALL) (1900—   ). Writer; friend of the Bloomsbury Group. Married Ralph Partridge.

RALPH [REGINALD] PARTRIDGE (1894—1960). Writer; worked for The Hogarth Press. Married, first, Dora Carrington; second, Frances Partridge.

WILLIAM ROBERTS (1895—1980). Painter. Briefly associated with Omega Workshops.

SIR JOHN ROTHENSTEIN (1891—   ). Art historian; writer; and Director of the Tate Gallery, 1938—64. Son of Sir William Rothenstein.

SIR WILLIAM ROTHENSTEIN (1872—1945). Painter and writer. Member of the New English Art Club. Friend of Roger Fry, although relations between them later became strained. Author of *Men and Memories*, 1931—3.

FRANK RUTTER (1876—1937). Editor and writer. Art critic of *The Sunday Times*.

GEORGE RYLANDS (DADIE) (1902—   ). Fellow of King's College, Cambridge. Worked for The Hogarth Press in 1924.

SIR JOHN TRESIDDER SHEPPARD (1881—1968). Classicist. Provost of King's College, Cambridge.

GERALD SHOVE (1887—1947). Economist. Fellow of King's College, Cambridge. Apostle.

WALTER RICHARD SICKERT (1860—1942). Painter and critic. A founder of the New English Art Club, and founder of the Fitzroy Group and the Camden Town Group.

MATTHEW SMITH (1879—1959). Painter. A friend of Duncan Grant and Vanessa Bell.

STEPHEN SPENDER (1909—   ). Writer and poet. Early work published by The Hogarth Press.

STEPHEN TOMLIN (1901—37). Sculptor. Married Julia Strachey, niece of Lytton Strachey.

HENRY TONKS (1862—1937). Painter. Professor at Slade School of Art, 1918—30.

IRIS TREE (1897—1968). Writer. Daughter of Sir Beerbohm Tree. Painted by Roger Fry, Duncan Grant and Vanessa Bell.

ROBERT CALVERLY TREVELYAN (TREVIE) (1872—1951). Poet and writer. Friend of Roger Fry; shared a house with him in the early years.

LALLA VANDERVELDE (1870—1964). Wife of Emil Vandervelde, Belgian Ambassador to London. Patron of the arts, and of the Omega Workshops. Friend of Roger Fry.

CHARLES VILDRAC (1882—1964). Poet, gallery owner and patron of avant-garde artists. Friend of Roger Fry, Duncan Grant and Vanessa Bell.

EDWARD WADSWORTH (1889—1949). Painter. Exhibited in Second Post-Impressionist Exhibition. Briefly associated with Omega Workshops; resigned with Wyndham Lewis.

ALLAN WALTON (1891—1948). Painter, textile designer and manufacturer. Produced fabrics designed by Vanessa Bell and Duncan Grant in the 1930s.

NATHANIEL WEDD (1864—1940). Fellow of King's College, Cambridge. A friend of Roger Fry at Cambridge.

EDWARD WOLFE (1897—1982). Painter, born in South Africa. Studied at the Slade School. Associated with Omega Workshops.

For fuller details, *see Who's Who in Bloomsbury*, Alan and Veronica Palmer, The Harvester Press, 1987.

LIST OF PLATES

LIST OF PLATES

LIST OF PLATES

LIST OF PLATES

LIST OF PLATES

LIST OF PLATES

SELECT BIBLIOGRAPHY

Anscombe, Isabelle — *Omega and After*, London 1981

Bell, Clive — *Art*, London, 1914
Pot-Boilers, London, 1918
Since Cézanne, London, 1922
Landmarks in Nineteenth Century Painting, London, 1928
Civilization, London, 1928
An Account of French Painting, London, 1931
Old Friends, London, 1956

Bell, Julian — *Essays, Poems and Letters* (ed. Quentin Bell), London, 1938

Bell, Quentin — *Bloomsbury*, London, 1968
Virginia Woolf (a biography), 2 Vols., London, 1972 (ed. with Garnett, A., Garnett, H. and Shone, Richard)
Charleston, London, 1987
Bad Art, London, 1989

Bell, Vanessa — *Notes on Virginia's childhood* (ed R.J. Schaubeck, Jr), New York, 1974

Collins, Judith — *The Omega Workshops*, London, 1984

Cork, Richard — *Vorticism and Abstract Art in the First Machine Age*, Vol 1, London, 1975

Edel, Leon — *Bloomsbury: A House of Lions*, London, 1979

Fry, Roger — *Giovanni Bellini*, London, 1899
Vision and Design, London, 1920
Duncan Grant, London, 1923
Transformations, London, 1926
Cézanne, London, 1927
Reflections on British Painting, London, 1934
Last Lectures, Cambridge, 1939

Fuller, Peter — *Theoria*, London, 1988

Garnett, Angelica — *Deceived with Kindness*, Oxford, 1984

Garnett, David — *The Golden Echo*, London, 1954
The Flowers of the Forest, London, 1956
The Familiar Faces, London, 1962

Holroyd, Michael — *Lytton Strachey, a Critical Biography*, 2 Vols., London, 1967–8

Johnstone, J.K. — *The Bloomsbury Group*, London, 1954

Kennedy, Richard — *A Boy at the Hogarth Press*, London, 1972; Harmondsworth, 1978

Keynes, John Maynard — *Two Memoirs*, London, 1949

MacCarthy, Desmond — *Memories*, London, 1953

Mortimer, Raymond — *Duncan Grant*, Harmondsworth, 1948

Partridge, Frances — *Memories*, London, 1981

Rosenbaum, S.P. (ed.) — *The Bloomsbury Group: a Collection of Memories*, London, 1975
Victorian Bloomsbury, London, 1987

Rothenstein, John — *Modern English Painters*, Vol. 2, London, 1956

Rothenstein, William — *Men and Memories*, 2 Vols., London, 1931–2

Shone, Richard — *Bloomsbury Portraits*, London, 1976

Sitwell, Osbert — *Laughter in the Next Room*, London, 1949

Spalding, Frances — *Roger Fry: Art and Life*, London, 1980
Vanessa Bell, London, 1983

Spender, Stephen — *World within World*, London, 1951

Stansky, Peter, and Abrahams, William — *Journey to the Frontier*, London, 1966

Sutton, Denys (ed.) — *The Letters of Roger Fry*, 2 Vols., London, 1972

Strachey, Lytton — *Eminent Victorians*, London, 1918

Tillyard, Stella — *The Impact of Modernism*, London, 1988

Todd, Dorothy, and Mortimer, Raymond — *The New Interior Decoration*, London, 1929

Watney, Simon — *English Post-Impressionism*, London, 1980

Woolf, Leonard — *Sowing. An Autobiography of the Years 1880 to 1904*, London, 1960
Growing. An Autobiography of the Years 1904 to 1911, London, 1961
Beginning Again. An Autobiography of the Years 1911 to 1918, London, 1964
Downhill all the Way. An Autobiography of the Years 1919 to 1939, London, 1967
The Journey not the Arrival Matters. An Autobiography of the Years 1939 to 1969, London, 1969

Woolf, Virginia — *The Diary of Virginia Woolf* (ed. Anne Olivier Bell and A. McNeillie). Vols. 1–5, London, 1977
The Letters of Virginia Woolf (ed. Nigel Nicholson), London, 1977
A Room of One's Own, London, 1929
Roger Fry: A Biography, London, 1940
Moments of Being (ed. Jeanne Schulkind), Sussex, 1976

CATALOGUES

Arts Council — *Vanessa Bell: A Memorial Exhibition*, London, 1964

Arts Council and Nottingham University — *Vision and Design: the Life, Work and Influence of Roger Fry* 1966

Collins, Judith, and Shone, Richard — *Duncan Grant, Designer*, Liverpool and Brighton, 1980

Cork, Richard — *British Art in the Twentieth Century*, London, 1987

Crafts Council — *The Omega Workshops*, London, 1984

d'Offay, Anthony — *Vanessa Bell: Paintings and Drawings*, London, 1973

D'Offay Couper Gallery — *Duncan Grant: Watercolours and Drawings*, 1972

Tate Gallery — *Duncan Grant: A Retrospective Exhibition*, 1959

Wildenstein Gallery — *Duncan Grant and his World*, 1964

UNPUBLISHED SOURCES

Bell, Vanessa — *Memories – Hyde Park Gate and Recollections of Roger Fry*, with the kind permission of Professor Quentin Bell and Angelica Garnett.

Charleston Papers — Selection from letters, memoirs, etc., in the Tate Gallery Archive

INDEX

ACKNOWLEDGEMENTS

Permission to reproduce the letters, memoirs and writings in this volume has been generously granted by many people, estates, publishers, agents, museums and archives. We would gratefully like to acknowledge first and foremost the extraordinary cooperation of Angelica Garnett and Professor Quentin Bell, together with Henrietta Garnett, The Tate Gallery Archive and the following:

Chatto and Windus/The Hogarth Press and the Executors of the Clive Bell Estate, the Executors of the Roger Fry Estate, the Executors of the Leonard Woolf Estate and the Executors of the Virginia Woolf Estate, as appropriate, for permission to quote from:

Clive Bell: *Art*, 1914 pp 250, 255
Clive Bell: *Since Cézanne*, 1922 pp 251, 254, 266
Clive Bell: *Civilization*, 1928 pp 255
Clive Bell: *Old Friends*, 1956 pp 23, 36, 153
Julian Bell: *Essays, Poems and Letters* (ed Quentin Bell), 1938 pp 148, 156
Roger Fry: *The Letters of Roger Fry* (ed Denys Sutton), 1972 pp 34, 35, 36, 50, 51, 52, 53, 54, 55, 56, 66, 67, 124, 125, 128, 129, 130, 131, 134, 135, 136, 137, 143, 150, 153, 257
Leonard Woolf: *Sowing*, 1960 pp 29, 38
Leonard Woolf: *Beginning Again*, 1964 pp 23, 42, 65, 66, 161, 164
Leonard Woolf: *Downhill All the Way*, 1967 pp 164, 165, 166, 167, 273
Leonard Woolf: *The Journey Not the Arrival Matters*, 1970 pp 168, 169
Virginia Woolf: *The Diary of Virginia Woolf*, (ed Anne Olivier Bell), 1977 pp 30, 142, 147, 151, 159, 161, 163, 164, 165, 166, 167, 169
Virginia Woolf: *The Letters of Virginia Woolf*, (ed Nigel Nicolson), 1976 pp 140, 147
Virginia Woolf: *A Room of One's Own*, 1929 pp 39
Virginia Woolf: *Memoir of Julian Bell*, 1937 pp 159
Virginia Woolf: *Roger Fry, a Biography*, 1940 pp 28, 34, 35, 50, 51, 53, 56, 58, 126
Quentin Bell, et al: *Charleston Past and Present*, 1987 pp 140

(US rights for the Leonard Woolf material and Virginia Woolf's *The Diary of Virginia Woolf*, *The Letters of Virginia Woolf*, *A Room of One's Own* and *Memoir of Julian Bell* are by kind permission of Harcourt Brace Jovanovich Inc.)

Hamish Hamilton Ltd for permission to quote from the following:
Gerald Brenan: *South from Granada*, 1957 © Gerald Brenan 1957 pp 272

A.P. Watt, on behalf of the Executors and Estate of David Garnett, for permission to quote from the following:
David Garnett: *The Golden Echo*, 1954 (US rights by kind permission of Harcourt Brace Jovanovich Inc.) pp 47
David Garnett: *The Flowers of the Forest*, 1956 pp 141, 144, 147

Grafton Books (a division of the Collins Publishing Group) for permission to quote from the following:
J.M. Keynes: *Two Memoirs*, 1949 pp 37

Longman Ltd and David Higham Associates for permission to quote from:
John Lehmann: *The Whispering Gallery*, 1955 pp 155

The Random Century Publishing Group for permission to quote from the following:
Wyndham Lewis: *Rude Assignment*, 1950 pp 134

The Granada Publishing Group and David Higham Associates for permission to quote from the following:
Desmond McCarthy: *Memories*, 1953 pp 36, 62

Penguin Books Ltd for permission to quote from:
Raymond Mortimer: *Duncan Grant*, 1944 © Raymond Mortimer 1944 pp 268